CANNABIS SATIVA

M000217758

The Essential Guide to the World's Finest Marijuana Strains

Edited by S. T. Oner
With an introduction
by Greg Green

Volume

1

GREEN CANDY PRESS

Cannabis Sativa:

The Essential Guide to the World's Finest Marijuana Strains, Volume 1

Published by Green Candy Press
San Francisco, CA
Copyright © 2012 Green Candy Press
ISBN 978-1-931160-93-3

Photographs © A.D., ACE Seeds, Advanced Seeds, Alphakronik Genes, Alpine Seeds, Andre Grossman, Anna, Apothecary Genetics, ASG Seeds, Autofem Seeds, BillBerry Farms, Blim Burn Seeds, Buddha Seeds, Cabin Fever Seed Breeders, CannaBioGen, Cannaseur Seeds, Centennial Seeds, Ch9 Female Seeds, David Strange, De Sjamaan, Delta 9 Labs, Dinafem Seeds, DJ Short, DNA Genetics, Don't Panic Organix, Dr. Atomic Seedbank, Dr. Canem and Company, Dr. Greenthumb Seeds, Dr. Underground, Dready Seeds, Dutch Passion, Ed Borg, Eddie Funxta, Emerald Triangle Seeds, Eva Female Seeds, Female Seeds, Finest Medicinal Seeds, Flying Dutchmen, Focus, Freak, Gage Green Genetics, Ganjah Seeds, Genetics Gone Madd, Giorgio Alvarezzo, Granpa G, Grass-O-Matic, Green Born Identity, Green Devil Genetics, Green Haven Genetics, Green House Seed Co., Green Life Seeds, Homegrown Fantaseeds, HortiLab Seed Company, HY-PRO Seeds, IceToker, JD Short of DJ Short Seeds, Jin Albrecht, Kaliman Seeds, Kannabia Seeds, Karma Genetics, Karmaceuticals LLC, Kingdom Organic Seeds by The Rev, Kiwiseeds, Low Life Seeds, Lowrider, M.Heinrich, Magus Genetics, Mandala Seeds, Ministry of Cannabis, MoD, Moonunit, Mosca Seeds, Mr. Nice Seeds, Mystic Artist, MzJill, Next Generation Seed Company, No Mercy Supply, North of Seeds, Ocanabis, Old Man's Garden, Original Seeds, OtherSide Farms, Paradise Seeds, Peak Seeds, Philosopher Seeds, Pistils, Pitt Bully Seeds, Poor White Farmer Seeds, Positronics Seeds, Project Skunkenstein, Queen Seeds, Redstar Farms, Reggae Seeds, Resin Seeds, Riot Seeds, Royal Queen Seeds, RYKA Imaging, Sagarmatha Seeds, Sannie's Seeds, Sativa Tim, Seedism Seeds, Sensi Seeds, Serious Seeds, Short Stuff Seeds, SinSemillaWorks!, SnowHigh Seeds, Soma Seeds, Southern Star Seeds, Spliff Seeds, Stitch, Subcool and Team Green Avengers, Sweet Seeds, T.H. Seeds, The Bulldog Seeds, The Original Sensible Seed Co., The Releaf Center, The Wizards of Oz, TreeTown Seeds, Ultimate Seeds, Underground Originals, Unidentified Wisconsin Grower, Vulkania Seeds, Weed.co.za, West Coast Sinsemilla, Whazzup, White Label Seeds, World of Seeds.

Cover photo: Green Crack is courtesy and Copyright © Giorgio Alvarezzo, West Coast Sinsemilla, and SinSemillaWorks!

This book contains information about illegal substances, specifically the plant Cannabis and its derivative products. Green Candy Press would like to emphasize that Cannabis is a controlled substance in North America and throughout much of the world. As such, the use and cultivation of cannabis can carry heavy penalties that may threaten an individual's liberty and livelihood. The aim of the Publisher is to educate and entertain. Whatever the Publisher's view on the validity of current legislation, we do not in any way condone the use of prohibited substances.

All rights reserved. No part of this book may be reproduced in any form without express written permission from the Publisher, except by a reviewer, who may quote brief passages or reproduce illustrations in a review where appropriate credit is given. Nor may any part of this book be reproduced, stored in a retrieval system, or transmitted in any form or by any means without written permission from the Publisher.

Printed in China by Oceanic Graphic Printing
Sometimes Massively Distributed by P.G.W.

Dedication

by S.T. Oner

"War does not determine who is right; only who is left."
— Bertrand Russell

As always, I wholeheartedly dedicate this book to the fine people at NORML and everyone who has fought against the unjust war on this incredible plant. It seems to me that the drug law revolution is creeping ever closer, and though it may be our nation's inability to curb its spending on war that leads to it eventually decriminalizing cannabis, and the irony of this will certainly not escape us, there will be no winners of the war on drugs; only people whose suffering will finally end.

Following the success of the first volume in this series, *Cannabis Indica: The Essential Guide to the World's Finest Marijuana Strains*, my thanks must go out to everyone who has been involved in any small part in this project. The public's reaction to the book was nothing short of astounding, so for this, I thank you all.

Once again, without the fantastic breeders and seed companies whose work appears between these pages, I would never have been able to accomplish such a mammoth task. This book features breeders from the USA, Canada, Holland, Britain, Spain, France, Germany, Switzerland, South Africa, Russia, Australia, Ukraine, New Zealand, and Belgium, and quite a few other countries which cannot be listed due to certain draconic laws against this most holy of plants.

There are some contributors who wish to remain anonymous, but who deserve recognition and respect nonetheless, as does everyone on the online forums, like the good people at Breedbay.co.uk, Meduser.ca, Riotseeds.nl and Seedfinder.eu

Finally I must thank the growers, breeders and writers who inspired me to learn more about this incredible plant; Ed Rosenthal, Jason King, Danny Danko, Mel Thomas, Mel Frank, Kyle Kushman, Greg Green, and Jorge Cervantes are some big ones, and of course the unforgettable Jack Herer, may he rest in peace. These guys are the pioneers of the movement and it is their work that set me out on my first steps of this wonderful journey. I feel that Cannabis Sativa Vol. 1 provides an accurate picture of the amazing variety of cannabis genetics in existence today. This book would not exist without the years of hard work and effort of everyone featured in it, and for this, I say thank you.

Contents

Preface

A Trip With Sativa

Welcome, friends, stoners, countrymen! Lend me your ears! I'm glad you made it. Are you comfortable? Then we'll begin.

I hope that some of you have found yourselves here after reading my first book in this series, *Cannabis Indica: The Essential Guide to the World's Finest Marijuana Strains, Volume 1*. Some of you might have been given this book by a friend, while others might have stumbled upon it in a bookstore and been intrigued by the cover. How you got here doesn't really matter. What matters is that you're here.

If you've read my first strain guide, you'll know that this series is a celebration of all things cannabis. In the first indica book, I compiled 100 of the best indica strains available today, and to do so I scanned the globe for the very best breeders and genetics. I found myself conversing with growers from never-thought-of places in small-town Russia and researching the origins of such big names as Hindu Kush and Blueberry in cities from Northern California to Northern India. I was honored to feature some small time but hugely talented personal growers throughout the USA and Europe, whose passion for the plant has resulted in some astounding hybrid strains.

Now, it's the time for sativa to step into the spotlight.

The sativa renaissance has, I think, been long overdue. As the culture of indoor growing has spread across the USA, sativa strains have had to take a backseat in the minds of many cultivators. While indica-dominant plants tend to grow small and bushy, the mighty sativa is often tall and leggy, going well beyond the tiny grow space that graces many a dorm room, closet or third-floor balcony these days. The opinion

Preface

that became prominent was that only indicas are suitable for indoor growing.

However, the last 20 years have seen some amazing leaps forward in both breeding and growing techniques that have made this claim obsolete. Hybridization of strains means that a mostly-sativa plant can have indica genes that curb its growth, while a supposedly small indica plant can shoot up in height thanks to the influence of sativa genetics. In a world where most strains are now hybrids, anything can happen! The Joint Doctor's Lowryder plant also threw a curveball by bringing ruderalis genetics into the game. Cannabis ruderalis has long been ignored by the cannabis community due to the species' inability to get you high. However, The Joint Doctor recognized that its auto-flowering capabilities would greatly benefit the indoor grower, and so bred his best indica plants with ruderalis varieties to create strains that not only stayed small and manageable, but needed no change in light cycle to get themselves to maturity. Recently, ruderalis plants have been bred with sativas, to create plants that enjoy shorter flowering times than pure sativas and also stay relatively small compared to their pureblood sisters. With such strains as Maxi Gom and some stellar auto-flowering AK-47 varieties on the market, indica's stronghold on indoor growing has been challenged.

The rise of more complex growing techniques has also turned more indoor growers on to sativa strains in the recent past. Whereas outdoor growing can be as easy as letting your huge plant get as wild as it likes, indoor cultivation may necessitate a little more ingenuity, especially if your plants are growing larger than your grow space. Although the Sea of Green (SOG) technique has been around for donkeys' years now, other processes such as LST, topping and FIM-ing have made indoor and outdoor sativa cultivation that little bit easier. LST, or Low Stress Training, focuses on how to

make your plant grow in a way that suits your grow space by careful use of string or twine, whereas both topping and FIM-ing (with the FIM standing for Fuck I Missed) deal with how to force your plant to create new growths that better suit your garden. All three of these methods can help growers to utilize the space that they have, whether that's 40 acres of greenhouse, a tiny closet or a 5x5 box room.

We often take it for granted that new techniques and technologies crop up repeatedly, and we pick and choose as to which new methodologies will benefit us. We shouldn't forget, though, that every new growing idea is the result of years of tireless effort by some innovative cultivator who, instead of keeping his creative styles to himself, shares his knowledge with the community so that everyone might find growing easier and more enjoyable. To those growers, we say Thank You.

Of course, outdoor growers have long enjoyed the pleasure of watching a crop of sativa plants grow into veritable monsters – and have enjoyed even more the final harvest and the piles upon piles of fresh, high-quality bud that these plants create. Breeders and commercial cultivators have long held the names of Diesel and Haze to be sacred, and everyday tokers often won't smoke anything but. The pure sativa Haze family in particular holds a special place in the hearts of all serious stoners, and whether it be a joint of the Super, Amnesia or Mekong type that you're smoking, you'll know the Haze high when it hits you: an almost psychedelic, soaring fantasy of a trip that takes you places that indicas never can. For me, however, it's the Diesel strains that are the real sativa stars. The strains in regular rotation in my stash include any variety I can get my hands on, with Denver Diesel and Soma's famous NYC Diesel being particular favorites. Within these pages, you'll find dozens of strains that might not have the Haze or Diesel tags in their names but still count themselves as extended

Preface

family. Breeders everywhere know the benefits of hybridizing Haze and Diesel with other varieties: from Amnesia to Sage 'n Sour, some of the best sativa strains come from these two superstars, somewhere along the line.

So why do sativa strains have such a revered following by the breeders and growers who smoke every single day? Well, my own experience can probably answer that question. When I was a mere whippersnapper, smoking my first blunts of Kush behind the high school walls, I used to struggle to look like the tough kid I so wanted to be when the strength of the indica strains would make my juvenile legs wobble like a newborn goat and I'd be dribbling down my own face. At that point, I didn't even know that there were different species of cannabis, let alone understand the differences between each one.

Several years later on a summer break from school, I was working part-time for a marine biologist in Venezuela when, after a particularly tiring dive and a slight case of the bends, one of the local guys passed me a joint of what I'd later find out was a landrace sativa from neighboring Colombia. Instead of falling asleep quietly in the corner as I expected to, I began talking and I couldn't stop. My mind was racing, my limbs felt light and my eyes were wide open in every sense of the word. I was feeling that sativa high for the first time, and man, did it feel good. I continued smoking with my friend and slid gloriously into that semi-psychedelic sativa high where everything in the world is dreamy and you're flying fast through its never-ending streets. My whole opinion of my already-beloved cannabis had changed for the better, and I never looked back.

Now, too many years later, I've found that wobbly legs and dribbling are an unavoidable part of the aging process, so I've made my peace with indica and enjoy the

odd face-melter on regular occasions. And yet it's still the sativa that I reach for when I wake up; still the sativa that gets passed around when the wine has been finished; still sativa that I grow in my backyard proudly for everyone to see. It gets me going for the day, keeps me pepped when coffee has become redundant, and it sets my brain alight when it's time to write. In fact, I'm smoking some very nice NYC Diesel right now.

It's because of this love for sativa that I've created Cannabis Sativa: The Essential Guide to the World's Finest Marijuana Strains, the only strain guide to feature 100 sativa strains from 100 different breeders from around the world, with high quality full-color photos to match. Once again, my heartfelt thanks go out to the breeders, seed companies, growers and cannabis lovers who are featured in this book, and without whom I could never have created something that I'm now so proud of. The great thing about the cannabis community is that the deeper you go, the better it gets, and though some of the underground breeders and growers preferred not to be name checked here, they should know that the help they gave me in putting this together will never be forgotten.

Whether you're already a "sativa diva," as some of my breeder friends say, or you're an indica lover curious about the other side, or even if you've only ever smoked some nameless pot that the weird dude on the corner gave you, I hope that you will find a new love within these pages, and will soon be a sativa convert much like myself.

Introduction

Just what is Sativa?
By Greg Green

Sativa is the archetype of the cannabis plant. When a cannabis leaf is used in a logo, 99% of the time it is a sativa leaf, and because of this, those long, thin, serrated blades scream "Cannabis!" to anyone who sees them. Yet very few modern cannabis users have genuinely ever grown or used pure sativa, but have been dealing with sativa hybrids instead. The dominance of sativa-dominant strains over pure sativas means that, in a way, many tokers are missing out on what is probably the best that the world of cannabis has to offer.

When extolling the virtues of sativa, it is important to remember that it is the genes of sativa plants that drive them to be so phenomenal. During the process of cellular meiosis involved in reproduction, these genes are recombined in various ways to allow for variation and diversity, but ultimately the sativa genetic code will undergo developmental biology, instructing itself on how to develop into a sativa plant. The fact that such a natural process can result in a plant that forms such a beautifully symbiotic relationship with humans is a wonder in itself; we tend to the plant and maintain its fabulous genetics, while it gets us crazy high and opens up our minds like never before. The sativa strains most well known for their mind-bending qualities have, over time, become the most sought-after varieties. You may already be aware of some of these strains, such as Cheese #1 (Kaliman Seeds), Amnesia (HY-PRO Seeds), Chem #4 (Green Haven Genetics), ChemDawg 1991 (Poor White Farmer Seeds; Breeder: Chemdog), Kaya 47 (Advanced Seeds), Durban Poison (Weed.co.za), and Amnesia Haze (Finest Medicinal Seeds).

Introduction

The genetic diversity that sativa gets through meiosis means that cannabis as a species varies and this is also true for the sativa subspecies. While there is a lot of uniformity between sativa strains there is also a lot of diversity and this allows breeders to create myriad different strains for the market. If you flick through the pages of this book you should be able to see the results of sativa variation and note the degree of differences that are present in plant size, leaf shape, calyx size, calyx amounts, calyx color and floral clusters. Of course, each different variety also gives a unique type of high, and it is this that makes the diversity of sativa strains so interesting for most smokers.

We've already discussed the differences in effect between sativa and indica, but for cultivators, the most notable differences between the two come across in how they grow. Sativa grows and flowers for much longer than indica. In some cases a grow season for sativa can be the better part of three quarters of a year from seed to harvest. In addition, sativa plants tend to be much taller than indica and sometimes several times so. While indica is often called a squat plant, sativa is known for being lanky, almost to the opposite extreme. This means that sativa in general is not a popular indoor strain but is very popular for greenhouse and outdoor grows. If sativa is grown indoors then the grower needs to have a lot of experience with tying down their plants or training them or else a very high ceiling. Having said this, there are strains emerging these days that manage a sativa's height by adding indica genetics, while still maintaining the sativa high that smokers so love.

It is easy to see why people who love growing sativa find it almost an obsession; to grow a plant that looks how cannabis *should* look is an amazing feeling. Add to this the fact that many old-school growers and smokers were first introduced to sativa strains and so are very passionate about maintaining their favorite sativa genetics to pass on to future generations, and you might truly understand why the cult of sativa is so strong, even now. However, cultivators that might be curious enough to grow pure sativa strains have to be aware that sativa grows are renowned for taking up much more grow time and grow space for possibly less quantity but very high quality. Genetics for sativa are therefore usually a little more expensive and many of the pure sativa varieties, to all intents and purposes, are not strains suitable for beginners but rather for quite experienced growers. It is also very difficult to grow a lot of sativa plants densely like in an indica SOG or ScrOG grow and generally sativas are kept well apart, maybe even using one light per plant. While historically cannabis sativa and cannabis indica share a common ancestor, there is strong evidence that sativa was the first type of cannabis to be introduced into Western culture. Given the difficulty of growing sativa, it is not surprising that domestic cultivation programs were not as efficient or as plentiful as they are today. Some sativa plants, especially outdoor plants, can actually get quite big, like a Christmas tree, with the lower side branches curving outwards and upwards so much that it appears that several plants are growing in the one spot.

Like indica, sativa can appear as a *landrace,* which means that some wild forms of sativa have been semi-domesticated by local breeders and growers. It is likely that sativas such as Thai or Cambodian are landraces that have been further bred and tamed for the strain market. This is why many growers may be surprised at finding a shorter than usual sativa strain that was advertised as sativa. Many breeders assign cannabis type to the high type and not necessarily the overall plant shape and characteristics. Probably the single most important thing a grower of sativa can do is to keep internode lengths as short as possible, as sativa internodes are quite long by nature, and indoors if the plant-to-light distance is not kept optimally these naturally long internodes can get very long, like several feet long and cause the plant to easily bend over. Sativa tends to bend naturally at the top anyway, especially at the end of flowering, but if you let those internodes get too long you could have a top cola on the floor. Almost all sativa growers will have to learn a sense of how to train their plants and tying up is certainly a must. Sativa is more a connoisseur plant for the indoor grower. More impressive sativa-influenced cannabis strains include AK-47 (Serious Seeds), NYC Diesel (Soma Seeds), Vortex (Subcool and Team Green Avengers), Sage 'n Sour (T.H. Seeds), Arcata Lemonwreck (Kingdom Organic Seeds by The Rev), and Psicodelicia (Sweet Seeds).

While a lot of the younger growers today might be more familiar with names like Kush than any sativa strains, almost all of the famous classic 70s and 80s strains are sativas. The most famous sativa of all time is the Haze family, with the most well-known variety possibly being Neville's Haze. If you're a thirty-year grower and toker, it's names like these that will excite you even now. With the resurgence of sativa's popularity, and the weight of the Medical Marijuana community finding sativa strains most useful in dealing with a whole array of medical problems, there are now many more commercial sativa-dominant hybrids than you could find ten or even five years ago. Today on the market you will come across some fantastic new-school sativa strains including sativa/indica hybrids like Kaligria (ASG Seeds), Guanabana (Blim Burn Seeds), The Magician (De Sjamaan), Mekong Haze (Delta 9 Labs), Moby Dick (Dinafem Seeds),

Introduction

Chocolope (DNA Genetics), Thai Lights (Dr. Atomic Seedbank), The Elephant Magic (Dr. Canem and Company), Jazz (Dr. Greenthumb Seeds), Crystal M.E.T.H. (Dr. Underground), Margoot (Green Devil Genetics), Eclipse (Homegrown Fantaseeds), and Azure Haze (JD Short of DJ Short Seeds).

Even as a sativa aficionado it can be difficult to recommend a sativa strain for the first-time grower or the best one to breed with, because sativa is anything but simple. Its complexity is exactly what makes this subspecies so thrilling and is why some growers refuse to grow anything but sativa throughout their whole growing careers. However, Thai and Haze strains do offer a good genetic basis to build from, although the chance of purchasing a pure sativa strain without any indica influence is pretty small these days. This is not to say that pure sativa strains are impossible to find, and growers from places such as South Africa and Hawaii are lucky enough to have such sought-after genetics right on their doorsteps. I would personally recommend the following sativa varieties for their popularity and purity: Australian Bushweed, Cambodian, Durban Poison, Haze strains, Malawi, Neville's Haze, Purple Haze, Swazi and Thai. From seeds of these strains you will be growing some of the old-school sativa and likely be closer to the purer forms that your parents used to smoke! Australian Bushweed is a popular strain in Australia, and the weed native to Cambodia is quite pure. Durban Poison, Malawi and Swazi are popular sativa strains grown in Africa. The Haze strains are hybrids, very popular to Dutch breeders and with origins likely in Nepal. All of these strains, though, are considered some of the most difficult one can grow.

As you can see, the 21st Century has seen a major sativa revival. This is likely due to better quality hybridizations making sativa more manageable. Instead of growing pure sativa, many indoor growers have been able to deal with "mostly sativa" or 50/50 "indica/sativa" hybrids. This is mainly because of indica, which was introduced and became popular in the 1980s. Indica allowed for easier indoor grow rooms and also the hybridization with sativa types to create less lanky plants. In a way hybridization allowed for sativa to be introduced into more indoor grow rooms and among more growers but just not in a pure sativa form. While Haze may be the pinnacle of sativa breeding, Thai may be the purest of the sativas available to potential breeders.

This revival is seeing a developing trend in both the number of growers trying sativa and the number of breeders who are increasing their stock lines with sativa hybrids. Causes for this range from some recent competition wins featuring sativa to desires for more than just conventional indica strains, so many breeders are involving

Introduction

themselves more in the sativa trend in the hopes of winning some important prizes and having their fantastic work recognized. Of course the largest inducement to producing more sativas and growing them is the cerebral psychoactive effects with very limited body stone. Many users enjoy the experience of being able to function and do things while their minds experience some bliss. For some, bliss might be an understatement. It is often sativa that reputedly surprises even some very seasoned users. One time I heard a very seasoned Australian grower suddenly comment on experiencing bright lights dazzling him everywhere. Sativa effects can be somewhat similar to a hallucinogenic experience at times.

Of course, if left to its own devices, sativa wouldn't be nearly as accessible to many growers as it is today, and for that, we have to thank the innumerable sativa growers and breeders who have, over the years, brought this most amazing plant into the grow rooms and gardens of those less experienced cultivators and into the stash bags of everyday smokers. As we've already seen, cultivation of sativas can often be more difficult than indicas, and to work with these plants for decades at a time demands a lot of effort. The seed turnover for sativa is not only lower in some cases but often flowering takes so much longer that seed production is much less than that of indica. Given the longer flowering times, breeders' plans to stabilize sativa strains are often more ambitious and harder to make a success – yet still these breeders keep on, because they truly love sativa. When it comes to outdoor crops, sativa has always been a very popular cannabis plant and has been and remains the most likely cannabis variety to be found in outdoor guerilla grows. Although some may say that sativa has been pushed to the sidelines by indica and ruderalis varieties in recent years, these people would be overlooking what has been a game-changing shift in growing and smoking styles over the last decade or so. Not only has sativa cornered the outdoor market, it is also making new impressions on the competition scene and, as always, offers a cerebral experience that is unmatched. Though indica has its fans and can be enjoyed by everyone, sativa has just as strong a following and surpasses indica with its psychedelic properties and the pure delight of its form. There is definitely a place for both indica and sativa in every grower's garden and every toker's stash. In saying that, the holy grail of experiencing cannabis is likely to be a sativa and Neville's Haze just may be the very one.

CANNABIS
SATIVA
The Strains

AK-47

A relatively small but influential seed company, Serious Seeds provide product to many of the Amsterdam coffeeshops and thanks to this, as well as their penchant for creating varieties that blow others out of the water, their strains have been much sought after. AK-47 is one of their most infamous strains, and for good reason; as well as being a complete knockout high it is parent to many modern strains, including the auto-flowering Cetme from Pitt Bully Seeds and Serious Seeds' own White Russian. AK-47 is a complex mix of Colombian, Mexican, Thai and Afghani genetics that only a master breeder like Simon from Serious Seeds could manage. It's one of the most well-known contemporary strains and one of the most hard-hitting – it's no coincidence that this strain is named after the most lethal rifle in the world.

It's a common misconception that the strongest or most famous strains are harder to grow, and AK-47 banishes this myth by being particularly simple to cultivate. It can grow in any environment but prefers indoor set ups, where it will grow out in 10 days from clone. These seedlings will only ever get to a medium height, making a lack of space no problem. Their growth is vigorous, however, and if you plan on topping you're going to need to give the plants some support as they mature. A flowering time of 60 days is usual, and from this you can harvest up to 500 grams per square yard of grow room. The compact nugs are a sight to behold, with a thick coat of crystals and hardly any leaves, and it'll be tough to keep your hands off them until they've properly cured!

Serious Seeds, Holland

Sativa-Dominant

Genetics: Colombian, Mexican, Thai and Afghani

Potency: THC 21%

seriousseeds.com

One thing to consider when growing this strain is that the closer your buds get to harvest, the more they will stink. And I'm not talking a bit of a stench in the hallway, I'm talking the neighbors in the next street getting high off the smell. Don't worry though, some carbon filters should sort that right out, but when you start your grow be aware that odor might be an issue and choose a grow space accordingly!

Like its namesake, AK-47 has very powerful effects, but rather than knocking you down brain dead, it will leave you with a nice, balanced high, affecting both head and body, although if you carry on toking you'll find yourself with a serious head high. It's definitely a one-toke-wonder, though, and even if you're a daily smoker you'll be left a little blown away by its potency. If only we could get the armies of the world to carry this AK-47 instead of the guns, there'd be a lot less death and a lot more discussion of the meaning of Pink Floyd lyrics.

Amnesia

You might not have heard of Hy-Pro, but you'll definitely have heard of Amnesia: one of the most well-known sativa-dominant strains in recent history. Curiously, it wasn't created by one of the big-named breeders, but a guy at a nutrient company who had the magic touch. A blend of Neville's Haze and Afghani genetics, Amnesia took the pot world by storm and continues to do so, with so many Amnesia crosses on the market that it's impossible to keep track.

Though Amnesia is an unfussy strain, it grows best in soil containers and doesn't like to get too dry, so be careful to keep it moist at all times. Outdoors, these plants can easily reach 10 feet, so don't plant them too early in the season if you want to tame them; planting later will limit their growing time in the vegetative stage. A breeder's tip is to keep the plants fairly cool, and be very careful when applying nutrients. Flowering time is 12 weeks indoors, and be sure to bring some friends around harvest time as these buds are a hell of a job to trim!

HY-PRO Seeds, Holland
Sativa-Dominant
Genetics: Neville's Haze
x Afghani
Potency: THC 18%
hy-pro.nl

All your hard work will pay off as a few puffs on a pipe of Amnesia will have you soaring, exuberant and alive. A few more puffs, though, and you might not even remember where you put the stash. Did I leave it in the fridge? What's your name again?

Amnesia Haze

Finest Medicinal Seeds are pretty serious in their dedication to the medical marijuana community in Canada. Not only do they produce the great mag *Treating Yourself,* which dispenses information and guidance about how to grow, use and find the best medical weed, but they also sell high-quality seeds to ensure that anyone can get hold of quality product in their own home. If that wasn't enough they also create some fantastic strains, one of which is Amnesia Haze. A cross between a Super Silver Haze plant and a Cambodian sativa, this strain comprises some amazing genetics and is much lauded for its strong medicinal qualities – as well as its ability to get you totally high!

Amnesia Haze is a particularly resilient strain and can be saved from a lot of rookie errors if they're dealt with quite quickly, so if you find that you've overwatered in the early stages, give the plant enough time to dry out and then get onto a normal watering schedule. The Cambodian parent plant of this strain is a landrace sativa, and the genetics of the plant mean that Amnesia Haze can grow very tall and leggy unless trained properly in an indoor grow. You might decide to grow this one outdoors though, as the extra room and increased growth will also give a heavier yield of up to a crazy 900 grams per plant, if optimum conditions are reached. That alone makes this a particularly perfect strain for production on a commercial scale. Indoors, you can still get a harvest of 800 grams per square yard of grow room if you give the plants lots of light, but extra effort might need to be expended to keep the plants manageable. In both scenarios, the flowering time will be around 10 weeks.

Finest Medicinal Seeds, Canada

Sativa-Dominant

Genetics: Super Silver Haze x Cambodian

Potency: THC 15%

finestmedicinalseeds.com

The name of this strain lets you know exactly what its effects will be; you really will find yourself in an Amnesia Haze. Not only will all short-term memory go on a little holiday without telling you or even leaving a note, but your own motormouth and boundless energy will make the whole evening go by in nothing short of a haze. The cerebral effects of Amnesia plants are second to none, and this strain has the added bonus of fighting depression and stimulating the appetite too, making it fantastic medicine for a whole range of problems. The psychedelic properties of the Cambodian parent plant come through if you overindulge, so if your interest in marijuana is only as medicine in the spiritual sense you can also find solace in this strain. Just remember to try and keep one foot in reality – or at least on the doorstep.

Angel Heart

Seed companies are only as good as the breeders they have, so by that maxim, Mr. Nice Seeds must be top of the table with Shantibaba, Howard Marks and Neville Schoenmaker on their team. As each one is an international cannabis celebrity, it's no surprise that Mr. Nice Seeds have long been lauded for the quality of their original strains. This exceptional sativa-dominant hybrid comes from Mango Haze, an amalgamation of Haze, Northern Lights #5 and Skunk #1 heritage, and Afghan Skunk, which is a cross between an Afghani indica plant and the fabulous Skunk #1.

Angel Heart, a joint project by Neville and Shantibaba, is an adaptable plant and will grow well in almost any set up, whether an indoor hydro grow, an organic garden, an outdoor set up or in a greenhouse. If you choose to have an indoor crop, allow 60 to70 days for flowering in order to get the very most out of this strain, and a vegetative period of 5 weeks is generally sufficient to get the results you want. As this strain is one that is noted for its flavor, consider growing organically to let the natural flavors and traits of the Afghani grandparent come through properly. If any fertilizers or nutrients are used, then growers must flush with distilled water for a minimum of 2 weeks prior to harvest to let the taste really come through. Only with the natural light and quality air of an outdoor grow will Angel Heart reach its aromatic best, though a darkening greenhouse will also suffice. In the Northern Hemisphere harvest will occur at the start of October, and in the Southern Hemisphere it should be mid-March. A yield of around 50 grams per square foot of grow room is average, although some phenotypes can produce a much greater weight.

Mr. Nice Seeds, Holland

Sativa-Dominant

Genetics: Mango Haze x Afghan Skunk

Potency: THC 18%

mrnice.nl

The breeders recommend flowering out a selected mother plant by way of clone, as keeping the seed mother to produce clones may increase the speed at which the plants flower. They also advocate the selection of certain phenotypes that appear, according to personal taste; whichever plants smell the most luscious to you should be the ones you keep – that's if you can bring yourself to let the other ones go.

This strain produces aromas so sweet that even candy will taste sour afterwards and it is close to perfect in flavor. It is incredibly complex and layered in taste, and though the dried buds smell almost buttery the smoke is very Hazy, with smoky tones of pine and pepper. After the first toke you'll be ecstatic at having grown such a great taster, and this will only be heightened by the long-lasting, motivating high that will probably have you germinating your next batch before the night is out!

Apollo Jack

No one could accuse Spain's Queen Seeds of being unadventurous; for their Apollo Jack strain they've taken some of the very best contemporary genetics and bred them together to create some sort of monster. And by monster, of course, we mean a killer plant. For this strain they started off with a cross between the legendary Northern Lights #5 and Apollo G-13, a hydro-loving cross between Afghani and Thai plants, and bred this with a Jack Herer/White Widow cross of fantastic stature.

With parental pressure like that, you might expect this strain to be nervous or rebellious, but in fact she grows with lots of confidence and style. After a few days of the 24/7 light cycle the seedlings will be growing well, and are keen to stretch into the light, so make sure your lamps aren't too far away from the soil. This is definitely a lady who can look after herself, and neither pests nor disease can easily take her down – she's got the immune system of a vegan ox and a stature to match. She'll fill out in the flowering stage and by the end of a 60-day period you should be able to harvest about 600 grams per square yard of grow room.

Queen Seeds, Spain

Sativa-Dominant

Genetics: (Northern Lights #5 x Apollo G-13 Sativa) x Jack Widow

Potency: THC 19%

queen-seeds.com

biotops.biz

You'll be stoked anyway after such a good harvest, but one little toke will send your serotonin levels sky-high (pardon the pun) and your body will instantly succumb to the wave of relaxation that you deserve after so much effort.

Apple Jack

Based in Holland, the Seedism Seeds collective knows the Amsterdam coffeeshop scene extremely well. Back in 2001, the guys realized that Apple Jack was really taking off, and when one of the parent plants died they thought the end was nigh for the strain. However, breeder Hazemaster brought to the collective his technique of "selfing," or self-pollinating, and Seedism used their Apple Jack cut to bring this great variety back to the seed game.

As pleasant to grow as it is to smoke, Apple Jack flowers quickly for a sativa-dominant and gives sizable yields in any environment. Flowering can be finished within 10 weeks, although a week or two more may help to bring out the fantastic flavors in the final smoke. As a cross between Jack Herer and a White Widow, Apple Jack has enough indica genes to make it manageable even in a smaller grow room, although some training and trimming might be necessary. Towards the end of the flowering stage the buds will become very large, so staking your plants earlier will help to control and support them later on.

Seedism Seeds, Holland

Sativa-Dominant

Genetics: Jack Herer x White Widow

Potency: THC 21%

seedism.com

After curing, the solid nugs will smell a little hashy, but when burning, the very distinctive taste is more fruity than oily. Apple Jack brings a definite trippy stone, during which your body will be too happy to move and the room will revolve around your head at whatever speed it sees fit.

Arcata Lemonwreck

The Rev, based in the USA, is a grower passionate about two things: organic pot grown with his True Living Organics method, and cultivating the best strains possible. The fantastically-named Arcata Lemonwreck was given to him in Northern California, and touted as a cross between Humboldt Trainwreck and Lemon Afghani – though he believes it is more likely a Humboldt Trainwreck plant that's mutated along the way.

This strain is currently clone-only and as such, isn't very tolerant to stress. She should be kept out of high heat and will need a lot of TLC in flowering, when you should pay special attention to her calcium levels. She'll grow to around 4 feet indoors and will need structural support to hold her buds in flowering — and you need to watch out for her turning hermie if she's been under pressure! Unless you're growing in California or an area very much like it, you should probably grow this indoors. The Rev recommends that you use an organic soil grow to get the best from your bud. You should get 30 grams of bud per gallon of soil mix used.

Kingdom Organic Seeds by the Rev, USA

Sativa-Dominant

Genetics: Humboldt Trainwreck

Potency: THC 18%

hempdepot.ca

After a 30-day curing period, these buds have a lemony taste and smell. It's hard to hold this in a bong due to the massive expansion in the lungs, but after it hits and you're stoned as hell, you won't even remember what a bong is.

Auto Lemon Skunk

Low Life Seeds, based in the UK, is a breeders' collective focusing on strains that encompass the auto-flowering properties of the Joint Doctor's famous Lowryder strain. This time, they have bred the plant with a lemon phenotype of the equally famous Skunk #1, which is arguably North America's most well known and sought-after bud. Generations of backcrossing has stabilized this Lowryder offspring and created a fantastic plant for any cultivator to work with.

Low Life's love for their Lemon Skunk clone mother has surpassed many relationships, and is now well past its fifteenth year. The lemon phenotype was discovered in 1994 and she has been grown every season since. This is an especially short sativa-dominant hybrid, rarely growing beyond a foot in size, and so is a very suitable plant for those who only have a limited space. The auto-flowering characteristics also make this a great choice for those short on not only space but time too, and in fact this should be considered one of the ultimate plants for any stealth grow. Once flipped into the flowering period, Auto Lemon Skunk will form a massive central cola with very minimal branching. The crop grows in a very uniform manner with symmetrical plants, and finishing in just 10 weeks from seed, she's largely trouble-free and can adapt to many different media, although she isn't suitable for planting directly into the ground.

Low Life Seeds, UK

Auto-Flowering Sativa-Dominant

Genetics: Skunk #1 (Lemon Phenotype) x Lowryder

Potency: THC 16%

seedsman.com

Be aware that Auto Lemon Skunk is susceptible to drying out and is intolerant to growing situations where its root space is restricted. To combat these concerns, ensure that in the first few weeks the soil is always moist to the touch, and transplant into larger containers when you think it is necessary. The more room the roots have, the greater the growth. Be sure not to overfeed, and take measures to protect against spider mites, as their commitment to getting at your poor Auto Lemon Skunk plants is as impressive as it is annoying.

While its auto-flowering trait may be the main reason to grow this strain, the main reason to smoke it is its gorgeous aroma with a high to match: a fantastically balanced blend of a speedy sativa high and an indica couch lock. This balance means that you can smoke Auto Lemon Skunk all day, and as long as you don't get too carried away and start rolling epic face-melters, you can coast through to nightfall on the lemony smoke with no problems at all.

Azure Haze

It definitely cannot be said that JD Short, son of superbreeder DJ Short, is living in the shadow of his father's work. With original strains such as this one, the shorter Short is showing that he has the potential to surpass his ol' pop and lead the way in creating phenomenal hybrids, like this one, Azure Haze. A blend of his father's famous Blueberry male and Silver Haze female cut from the Bay Area, this sativa-dominant strain is much like Blue Dream, but is one generation closer to the Blueberry landrace generation.

Like its Silver Haze parent, Azure Haze exhibits very uniform growth patterns and a shorter stature than many sativa-dominant plants, making it a great choice for indoor or greenhouse cultivation. This is an interesting plant that might best suit a grower with some experience. The breeder suggests a flowering time of 9 to 10 weeks, and a long curing process will bring out the flavors even more, so try to keep your hands off your stash.

Haze has been called one of the most powerful pure sativas in the world, and the strength of the high certainly has been preserved through the generations. The taste of blueberry fruit gives way to a deeply cerebral and hard-hitting high that tends towards the psychedelic and shows why this strain is going to command a lot of attention.

JD Short of DJ Short Seeds, Canada

Sativa-Dominant

Genetics: Silver Haze x Blueberry

Potency: THC 17%

legendsseeds.com

greatcanadianseeds.com

Biddy's Sister

With over two decades of cultivation experience, the guys at Holland's Magus Genetics certainly have a few tricks up their sleeves. Noticing that their Biddy Early strain may be too big for some indoor growers, they created her "little" sister by crossing Early Skunk with Sensi Star, resulting in a plant much like Biddy Early but much smaller in stature and therefore much more suited to smaller indoor set ups while still retaining the beautiful flowers and powerful high.

This plant was created with indoor growers in mind, so she needs much less room than her big sister and responds very well to being put into a SOG situation. If you do choose to plant her outdoors, however, or give her an extra long vegetative period, she will bloom into a huge, bushy tree up to 8 feet tall. When moved into the flowering stage she'll develop a very strong and sweet aroma, which is delicious to behold, but also means that proper venting will be needed to eliminate smells that could give you away.

When the time comes for your first smoke of Biddy's Sister you're in for a treat: both sweet and minty, the taste recalls good Moroccan hash. The effects are just as good: a nice mind buzz and a relaxing body stone, but one mild enough to keep you moving, even if you do go quite slowly for the rest of the day.

Magus Genetics, Holland

Sativa-Dominant

Genetics: Early Skunk x Sensi Star

Potency: THC 17%

seriousseeds.com

Big Band

Spain's Kannabia Seeds are an energetic company forever bettering their product by stabilizing their existing strains and offering more new ones to the market. By crossing a special Bubble Gum plant with a hefty sativa from down California way, the guys and girls at Kannabia have produced a very Skunk-like plant that delivers a wicked buzz with a mouthwatering taste.

A definite indoor strain, Big Band is one of those plants that anyone can grow, from beginners to the experts and everyone else in between. The plants will form a large central cola but are resistant to changes of temperature and humidity, meaning that you're unlikely to lose any of those gorgeous buds to mold. She is unfussy and doesn't command a lot of attention, so as long as you keep her well fed and under good light, you should enjoy a fairly heavy harvest after an 8-week flowering period.

For such an easy-growing strain, Big Band has a very interesting smoke; the explosion of the Bubble Gum sweetness gives way to a menthol tang, brought about by the California Desert Sativa genetics. While you're reveling in this, the high will sneak up behind you and refuse to leave you alone for the next few hours, so you might as well make friends with it and enjoy each other's company. I'm sure you will.

Kannabia Seeds, Spain

Sativa-Dominant

Genetics: Bubble Gum x California Sativa

Potency: THC 10-15%

kannabia.es

Bigger Pine x Haze

The Original Sensible Seed Company were at the forefront of the European growing scene back in the early 90s, and after becoming frustrated with growing the coffee shop weed on offer in Amsterdam, began breeding their own strains, such as this one. Their Bigger Pine variety is a highly stable and very productive plant, while Haze is an incredibly popular pure sativa variety that is slow to grow but much lauded for its positive effects.

As parent plant Bigger Pine comes from inbred lines of Big Bud and Super Skunk, this strain has a very rich genetic history and delivers on all levels. Extensive back-crossing of this plant with the already stabilized Bigger Pine mother means that Bigger Pine x Haze is a particularly stable strain that will give very uniform crops – don't be shocked if your plants look like a little (or big!) marijuana army. The Haze genetics do bring a stretch to the plants so the more space you can give them, if growing outdoors, the better.

When smoked, this variety has a very distinct taste, with layers of fruits, pine and that indescribable Haze flavor that might leave you struggling for words. However, it's the high that's most impressive – an intense, cerebral treat that will rush in without knocking you over and then mellow out for a long-lasting and delightful stone.

The Original Sensible Seed Company, Spain

Sativa-Dominant

Genetics: Bigger Pine x Haze

Potency: THC 18%

original-ssc.com

Black Maui

USA-based breeder Snow has created a phenomenal strain with this great Hawaiian cross. Back in 2009, Snow took a clone of Maui Wowie, thought to be from Eddy Lepp's 1976 stock, and grew it to breed with The Rev's Maui-Wowie based Black Forest. This double dose of Hawaiian genetics makes Black Maui more islander than Duke Kahanamoku himself.

This strain has the enhanced vigor of a hybrid and is a very large plant when in its full glory. It has the telltale Christmas-tree shape with tons of branches, each of which has a good amount of bud sites. Flowering time is somewhere between 11 and 14 weeks. For such a strong sativa-dominant strain, the buds are liberally coated with resin, making them quite a joy to harvest. The huge colas smell sweet and spicy with a mild hint of citrus, making it difficult not to go a little mad and try to eat them while they're curing.

When you smoke up your first Black Maui you'll be treated to a very trippy type high with a lot of cerebral activity that is long lasting and energetic. For the more nervous smokers, this can result in heart palpitations and paranoia, though this is rare and can be dealt with easily – just keep some good friends and chill tunes around you. Black Maui is a gorgeous smoke and one that will be seriously twisting your melon, man.

PHOTOS BY SNOWHIGH

SnowHigh Seeds, USA
Sativa-Dominant
Genetics: 1976 Maui
Wowie x The Rev's Black
Forest
riotseeds.nl

Blue Geez

Blue Geez is a killer strain that originated in the Sierra Nevada mountains in Northern California, courtesy of the fantastic Cabin Fever Seed Breeders. This strain comprises many different varieties, as parent strain Empress Kush is a blend of three fantastic plants: ChemD, Loompa's Headband and Loompa's OG. This hybrid was then bred with a clone of Blue Cheese in 2010, making Blue Geez quite the little starlet with an attitude to match.

Depending on how long she's left to veg for, Blue Geez can reach up to 6 feet in height, although if you're into short women she can be kept to as little as 2 feet. She's unfussy about most other things, and will grow happily in both hydro and soil set ups as well as SOG. She's very resistant to both pests and disease, and if you keep her all natural treat her to a compost tea once in a while, you'll definitely be rewarded.

The final product from Blue Geez plants will be very dark, with purple and black tones amongst the brownish buds. The smell, too, is quite dark, being earthy and stinky with a hint of berries that makes the whole thing a lot more appetizing. The real kick, though, is in the high: a nice balance of head and body stone with just enough energy to keep you off that couch while still being great for medical use.

PHOTOS BY FREAK

Cabin Fever Seed Breeders, USA

Sativa-Dominant

Genetics: Blue Cheese clone x Empress Kush (ChemD x Loompa's Headband/Loompa's OG)

Potency: THC 17%

cannacollective.co.uk

thcfarmer.com/forums/f165

Bubble Fuck

For such a massive country, Australia is often horribly ignored by the North American and European seed communities. It's almost as if no one in the Pacific smokes pot. However, this is simply a huge misunderstanding on our part, and Southern Star Seeds are flying the flag for their beautiful sun-soaked country with this fantastic sativa. Bubble Fuck might sound like the result of a randy night in the tub, but it is in fact a result of a Bubble Gum F3 male and an Alaskan ThunderFuck F2 female getting a little hot under the collar and then giving birth to a little star of a baby.

Much like the never-aging Kylie Minogue, this plant hails from Victoria and first appeared to the world in 2008 – the plant, that is, not the tiny singer. We all know Kylie has been around since time immemorial. Though it's not as small as its weeny bopper sister, it doesn't grow that tall for a sativa, topping off at just under 6.5 feet, even outdoors. If you prefer your plants shorter, you can trim and tame Bubble Fuck to stay more manageable, but where's the fun in that? It's also an unfussy strain, suiting hydro and SOG grows as much as soil ones, and demanding no special feeding requirements, though it might appreciate listening to The Locomotion from time to time. For optimum results, however, the breeder recommends growing this plant outdoors in an organic medium, where both the synthetic-free situation and the fantastic natural airflow will see the plant grow to its strongest. After forced flowering Bubble Fuck will take a full 9 weeks to properly mature, but this is often the case with sativas, and nothing this good should ever be rushed. You can expect to harvest 200 grams from a single plant, but since this strain is currently only part of a private breeder's collection, you'll need to be lucky enough to get a clone first! Surely flights to Australia can't cost that much?

Southern Star Seeds, Australia

Sativa-Dominant

Genetics: Bubble Gum x Alaskan ThunderFuck

Potency: THC 15-17%

riotseeds.nl

If you do find yourself in the land of AC/DC (and there's actually a street named after them in Melbourne, just in case you weren't sure where you were) follow your nose when you smell the woody, hash-like smoke and you might just end up finding some nugs of Bubble Fuck. The high is very clear, very happy and incredibly creative, which might go some way to explaining the stereotype of Australians as very chilled out and extremely friendly. Just watch out on the creativity front or you might be coming up with some crazy Kylie-AC/DC mash up that embarrasses the good name of Australia.

Caribe

CannaBioGen has carved out a fantastic reputation for themselves thanks to their dedication to their work and their spectacularly reliable genetics. Their sativa-dominant Caribe strain is a triple-whammy of phenomenal genetics, as it is a backcross between their most resilient sativa from the Blue Mountains of Jamaica and an award-winning Northern Lights #5 / Haze cross.

This plant is a dream for indoor growers, as it is both high yielding and relatively small. The stature can be attributed to the Northern Lights #5 influence, as can the dense, dank buds that grow with impressive vigor from the very start of flowering. Even in more humid climates, Caribe shows a high resistance to all pests and problems. Breeders recommend that you subject the crop to a minimum of 30 days in the vegetative stage, to ensure optimum performance, followed by a 70 to 80 day flowering period. There should be no need for concern about odor control even in the latter stages of flowering; though these plants do give off a pleasant aroma it is nowhere near the Skunk-style permeating stink that gets in your clothes and hair and screams to everyone in the area "I AM GROWING POT." However, you may notice that as the buds begin to get more dense and heavy, the plant's branches will strain under their weight and start to droop. At the first signs of this happening, you should stake these suffering branches to help them hold the weight – you certainly don't want the branches to snap or the plants to fall over altogether. Another breeder's tip is to shorten the light period incrementally from 12 to 8 hours in the final 2 weeks of flowering, to augment resin production and stop the re-flowering that is common in many sativa-dominant hybrids. If you're growing outside this may not be an option, but by this point in the grow outdoor cultivators will be so taken with their beautiful plants and the thrilling amount of buds they're carrying that they won't be too concerned.

CannaBioGen, Spain

Sativa-Dominant

Genetics: Jamaica x Jamaica/Northern Lights #5/Haze

cannabiogen.com

If you manage to keep your hands off those delicious-looking flowers for the full 80 days of flowering, then give a full 2 weeks to the curing process, you'll find yourself enjoying a ridiculously clear and sharp Caribe high from the first toke. Your senses are heightened and colors seem clearer; even time seems to be at the mercy of your whims. You'll feel a slight body tingle to remind you of the indica influence, but this smoke is sativa in every other way, and you'll coast through on that head high for a good long while until it deposits you gently back down to earth and you start packing the next bowl.

Carnival

The breeders at Holland's Ministry of Cannabis (and where else would such a ministry exist?) have over a decade of experience cultivating cannabis, so they know good genetics when they see them. They've picked two fantastic plants to breed together, a mother from the ever-popular Haze strain and a beautiful sativa hybrid father, to create Carnival.

With its roots in Spain, this strain enjoys a climate similar to that of the Mediterranean if grown outside, although it is just as happy to be grown indoors, as long as you give it a lot of water with a pH of 6. It will only reach about 3.5 feet in height, which is very small considering its sativa dominance, and likes a flowering time of around 9 weeks with harvest coming 63 days after forced flowering. The breeder recommends that you give her 2 full weeks of flushing before harvest to retain the excellent flavor, and notes that Carnival can take high levels of fertilizer, and sometimes will need an extra dose of magnesium. These actions can help you harvest up to 50 grams of clean, tasty bud per square foot of indoor grow space.

Ministry of Cannabis, Holland

Sativa-Dominant

Genetics: Haze x Sativa Hybrid

Potency: THC 23%

ministryofcannabis.com

This strain is so named as it brings the carnival spirit to your mind. As the spicy, citrus-flavored smoke clears you'll feel energetic, uplifted, and free. You might even find yourself hunting out some cotton candy.

Cash Crop x Hawaiian

African cannabis genetics are very underused in the U.S., so it's great to find a German strain that comprises not just one set of African genes, but three! Breeder Granpa G over at Old Man's Garden has created this extremely rare and impressive Cash Crop x Hawaiian strain with three sativas from Ghana, Namibia and Malawi.

This is a strain for the connoisseur smoker and the expert grower. With an unruly plant like this that can grow up to 13 feet outdoors, you need a good amount of growing experience behind you to harness its real potential. Though this plant can be grown indoors, only with an outdoor grow can you get the mad harvests of a massive 700 grams per plant. If you do grow indoors, the breeder recommends cutting the light period down to 11 hours after 60 days of flowering, which causes maturity to be reached in about 90 days. After forced flowering you'll have to wait a full 12 to 14 weeks before your gorgeous buds will be ready to cut. Be armed with plenty of water, as these Fräuleins like to drink. They are also almost totally resistant to mold and frost and have a very high calyx-to-leaf ratio.

The effects of this strain are unbelievable; a crystal clear, soaring majesty of a high with a stimulating raciness that feels like speed. So achtung, baby, because this strain is hot!

PHOTOS BY GBI

Old Man's Garden;
Breeder: Granpa G,
Germany
Sativa-Dominant
Genetics: Ghanaian
Sativa x Namibian Sativa
x Malawian Sativa x
Hawaiian Indica
Potency: THC 18%

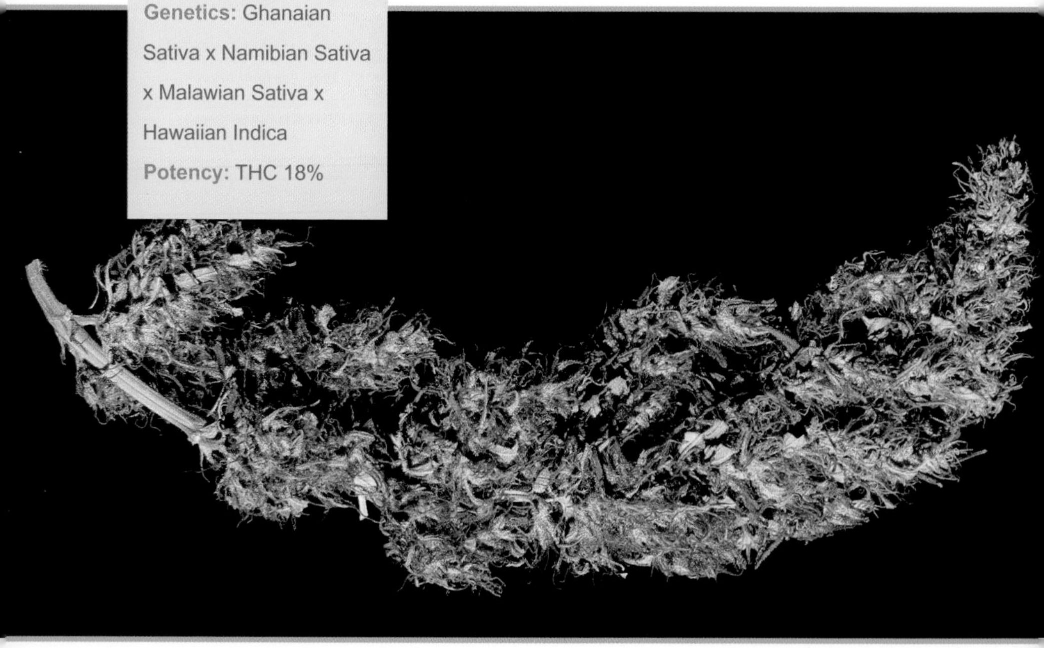

Cetme

Pitt Bully Seeds are a Spanish company with a fantastic range of both feminized and auto-flowering strains available. Cetme, which means "rifle" in Spanish, began life as an AK-47 plant from Serious Seeds. AK-47 is a mostly-sativa strain that has Colombian, Thai, Afghani and Mexican heritage and has become known worldwide for its quality – and because it shares its name with Mikhail Kalashnikov's most famous invention. The breeders then crossed this plant with an equally impressive ruderalis variety to give it auto-flowering traits, and in doing so took an already fantastic plant and made it much easier to cultivate.

Born after years of study, research and experimentation with the AK-47 parent and different breeding techniques, Cetme is a definite all-levels plant and can be grown by all growers. In comparison, AK-47 is known to be a strain best suited to those with more knowledge of growing pot, so if you're one of those people who can kill a Tamagotchi in under 48 hours then Cetme might be a better choice for you. After the seeds have sprouted and have grown into small seedlings, they should be planted directly into pots of around 6 or 7 liters with good quality soil. Be careful not to water them too much in the vegetative stage – the soil should be mostly dry before you water them each time. Once she's flipped herself into flowering (and because this is an auto-flowering variety, no change of light cycle will be necessary) you can increase the watering schedule to a more usual level. At this stage the plants can also deal well with nutrient feeding, although if they have shown weak growth in the vegetative stage, a clean water feed would be best.

Pitt Bully Seeds, Spain

Auto-Flowering

Sativa-Dominant

Genetics: AK-47 x Unknown Ruderalis

Potency: THC 16-19%

pittbully.com

laabuelaverde.com

Cetme's vegetative stage will last for 40 days with a similar flowering time, and the plant will not grow beyond 2 feet, which makes this one of the most compact sativa-dominant varieties available. This is great news for closet growers who might be tiring of their indica-dominant stash! Although the small stature does compromise the size of harvest somewhat, you should be able to get a healthy 40 grams from each plant.

Much like the AK-47, Cetme is a one-hitter strain that can debilitate the newbie smoker and will absolutely delight your hardcore potheads. Be sure not to tell your friends how easy it is to grow though – let them think you're an expert grower while they're tripping out on how good your stash is!

Cheese #1

UK-based Kaliman Seeds are onto a winner with their flagship baby Cheese #1, which is derived solely from the 1989 UK Exodus Cheese clone. This came about whilst the breeder, Rockster, was working on an Exodus Cheese x Skunk #1 cubing project which produced a strain with a very strong cheese-dominant taste combined with a marked citrus component from the Skunk #1 father. During this work a tray of twenty Exodus clones was put into flower and oddly two of these clones grew out as perfectly normal 100% looking males!

The resulting pollen was used to dust sister Exodus clones and when the seeds were grown out, every pheno produced bud that was indistinguishable in blind taste tests from the original. Cheese #1 is a light to medium feeder, finishes in 8 to 11 weeks, and gives an average yield. There are four main morphological phenotypes, although all are identical in chemotype/resin profile to the original. There is a short, more squat indica type that finishes fully in 56 days, with the more sativa types taking up to 11 weeks.

Kaliman Seeds, UK

Sativa-Dominant

Genetics: Original Cheese

Potency: THC 16%

kaliman.co.uk

Anyone who was lucky enough to smoke the original UK Exodus Cheese back in the 80s will find themselves transported back, as it is supposedly exactly the same dank, heavy taste as that original plant. Just try to avoid hitting the 80s fashions again. That's just not cool.

Chem #4

There is a lot of potlore that surrounds Chem #4. Some say it was the fourth and most glorious pheno from a set of bagseed in a $500 ounce that Chemdog bought at a Grateful Dead concert back in the day. Whether or not this is true, I can't say. However, I can say that this Green Haven version is the product of a 1991 ChemDawg clone and an OG Kush plant from the San Fernando Valley.

This strain has a good dose of indica influence and is thus pretty enjoyable to grow. You'll notice some wonderful internode formations and deep green leaves that will stay that way if you give her lots of light. Chem #4 is happy to live in a range of grow set ups, but you will get the most full natural flavor and high from an organic grow with minimal nutrients. Near the end of the flowering period this strain might need some additional assistance holding herself up, so it can be a good idea to plant stakes in the vegetative period so they're all ready to go when you need them.

The Chem #4 smoke is pretty serious, but has the gorgeous trait of not building much of a tolerance. It medicates both head and body, with anxiousness being dissolved away just as much as any physical pain. This makes it a great medical strain for those with mild depression as well as those with illnesses like Crohn's disease and arthritis.

Green Haven Genetics, USA

Sativa-Dominant

Genetics: 1991 ChemDawg x San Fernando Valley OG Kush

Potency: THC 17%

greenhavengenetics.com

ChemDawg 1991

Every generation has their big question. In the 60s, it was "Did man really land on the moon?" In the 80s it was "Who shot J.R.?" In our generation, it's "Where the hell did ChemDawg actually come from?" One of the most enigmatic strains of recent times, this sativa-dominant strain bred by Chemdog – and yes, that's the proper spelling - has more different backstories than David Bowie has characters. Some say it's a cross between Sour Diesel and OG Kush, others say Nepali x Thai, and some say it's the original Diesel, but the most accepted story is this: the original ChemDawg seeds came from a $500 bag of pot bought at a Grateful Dead concert at Deer Creek Amphitheater in 1991. The breeder popped these four seeds, and after the first turned out male and was disposed of (I know, dang), the second became the now legendary ChemDawg 1991. This strain really has become like gold in the weed world, and whenever anyone claims to have a cut of it or even a stash of buds, they're subjected to a hefty inquisition and forced to share. If you get some, and you don't want it to disappear in a day, keep it under your hat!

Poor White Farmer Seeds; Breeder: Chemdog, USA

Sativa-Dominant

Genetics: Unknown (Possibly: Nepali x Thai)

Potency: THC 21%

ChemDawg 1991s are fairly easy plants to grow, maturing after 10 weeks and flowering into huge colas. The main problem is that this strain is so sought-after that people tend to get a bit too worried about their plants and overwater them. Just chill, and let the plants do their own thing! The density of the final buds can mean that extra ventilation is needed in the grow room to ensure that mold doesn't form in the warm middle of the colas. You should also take preventative action against powdery mildew, as this strain can be susceptible to it. An extensive flush will help you get the best quality final buds without any chemical residue, because if you've been lucky enough to grow this bad boy, you don't want to ruin it on the homestretch.

All the folklore and mystery surrounding this strain is probably due to the fact that anyone who's smoked it can no longer remember their own name, let alone who they bought seeds from and what happened in 1991. This is a massive hitter and a serious contender for the World's Most Fucked-Up High. To say it's a heady stone would be missing something, as it's an all-over-body effect that sets your brain on fire. They say you'll know if you're smoking the real ChemDawg, and you probably will – but you won't know anything else!

Cherry OG

It's universally agreed by everyone over thirty that things were better in their day, so any older cannabis cultivators will absolutely love California's Emerald Triangle Seeds. They specialize in revamping some incredible traditional strains from back in the glory days, combining all the benefits of modern breeding techniques with proven varieties that everyone always loved. Cherry OG is an F1 cross between a Cherry sativa from the coast of Thailand and a Lost Coast OG plant. Lost Coast OG is an indica-dominant hybrid of Pakistani Kush, Lemon Thai and ChemDawg #4 design known to be a fast finisher, and much sought-after in California, especially with medical patients.

The parent strains of Cherry OG were chosen specifically to create a plant that gave tasty and dense flowers. To achieve this the breeders at Emerald Triangle crossed the Cherry Thai with an old Afghani indica plant to ensure good density and fast finishing times. Then they backcrossed the first offspring several times to bring out the flavors and the soaring high that made the Cherry Thai mother so popular. Finally, they introduced this plant to their own Lost Coast OG for increased potency and a sour taste to complement the fruity taste of cherries. The resulting plant enjoys very vigorous growth and grows tall and lanky with fairly thin branches. Though a variety of grow scenarios suit this strain, it performs best with a regular intake of additional nitrogen, calcium and magnesium that will ensure a strong green finish. Harvest will come after 10 weeks of flowering indoors or at the start of October outdoors, and depending on how much you have nurtured your plant, you can expect a yield that can be slightly higher than average or absolutely huge. Three phenotypes can be expressed, including a Sweet Cherry pheno and one with a Sour Diesel flavor.

Emerald Triangle Seeds, USA

Sativa-Dominant

Genetics: Cherry Thai x Lost Coast OG

Potency: THC 18%

emeraldtriangleseeds .co.uk

The smoke of Cherry OG will whisk you straight back to the 70s when Free Love was rampant and counterculture meant more than wearing a designer T-shirt with Che Guevara's face on it. The uplifting and motivating high will make you feel that the world is your oyster, life is glorious, and even though you might not be able to move from this couch for the next hour or so, that's okay because it is the most comfortable place in the world. Keep a pen and a piece of paper nearby and you might just write the new hot novel or comic book, or you could just veg out and theorize about the *Star Wars* movies with your friends. Either will be the best thing you've ever done.

Chocolope

Amsterdam-based DNA Genetics are amongst the forerunners in Holland's ever-flour-ishing cannabis industry, and their Chocolope is the result of an unholy union between OG Chocolate Thai female and Cannalope Haze male, both from DNA Genetics.

Originally named D-Line, Chocolope is a sativa-heavy hybrid and behaves ex-actly as you would expect her to. She likes to grow particularly tall, and is ridicu-lously easy to grow, making her best suited to an outdoor grow where you can give her the space she enjoys. Before being released to the public, this strain was back-crossed to get shorter flowering times, and now the plant has a flowering period of 8 to 9 weeks and yields around 50 to 60 grams per square foot. Don't harvest before the 12-week mark if you want to enjoy the best of the chocolate flavor. As the flow-ering period progresses you'll notice the nugs getting heavier and heavier, and as she won't have as much structural strength as a short indica plant, you might need to help her out by staking some of the branches.

DNA Genetics, Holland

Sativa-Dominant

Genetics: OG Chocolate Thai x Cannalope Haze

Potency: THC 18%

dnagenetics.com

Just one short puff is enough to get you hooked on this chocolatey smoke that is both rich and tasty. The high is very cerebral and almost trippy, so all in all, this is a fantastic strain; from growing to smoking, she deliv-ers on every level.

Claustrum

I'm a bit of a sucker for things with smart names, so I'm considering asking Positronics to marry me. Not only is their company named for the positronic brains that gave robots consciousness in 1940s sci-fi stories by Isaac Asimov, this strain is also named after a small sheet of grey matter in the human brain – a double-whammy of quiz show winning factoids. But there's more to Claustrum than a fantastic name - the presence of Kali Mist, Super Silver Haze and the legendary Jack Herer in its gene pool should be more than enough to prove that, even to the most hardened of cynics. The breeders first crossed Super Silver Haze and Kali Mist, which was then brought up right and introduced to the great Jack Herer strain.

The resulting Claustrum plants are very vigorous in their growth style and aren't shy about it. They'll grow quite tall in the vegetative period, even without any additions from you. However, they do enjoy a large amount of fertilizer and have good nutrient tolerance. While an indoor Claustrum plant can be kept to around a comfortable 3 feet with a little training and chopping, outdoors is a whole other ball game. Left to grow on their own with plenty of light, these guys can reach up to 16 feet tall – which, to put a little perspective on it, is the same height as two and a half Kobe Bryants standing on each other's shoulders. Such a massive plant can be a nightmare to deal with, but with a little support from staking and the extra strong stems that the wind will give them, your plants should stay strong and lively. You'll also find that this extra effort is worthwhile when it rolls around to harvest time and you find yourself pulling 600 grams off each of these monsters; though you might want to call some backup for the trimming session.

Positronics Seeds, Spain

Sativa-Dominant

Genetics: (Kali Mist x Super Silver Haze) x Jack Herer

Potency: THC 21%

positronicseeds.com

You'll notice just before harvest that Claustrum buds look a little different to what you're used to. This is because, with the right conditions, this strain will exhibit foxtailing, where you find little 'horns' or turnouts on the bud, making it look somewhat spikey. This is not a problem, and in fact it is a rare genetic trait that makes almost-finished nugs look even more badass. Once said nugs are cured, you will enjoy a gorgeous taste of pine and eucalyptus and an aroma that is pure Haze. The high, too, is a definite sativa: strong, heady, euphoric and stimulating. If you harvest at the right time your smoke will also be quite psychedelic, so don't be alarmed if your pipe turns blue and starts to melt in your hands.

Crystal M.E.T.H.

Naming your strain after America's most abused drug makes quite a statement, and Spain's Dr. Underground has done just that with Crystal M.E.T.H. Created by crossing CannaBioGen's Destroyer with Critical + (Bilbao cut), this is a true Spanish invention which, with those parents, was always going to be a heavy hitter.

Perfect for ScrOG set ups, this strain will give a higher than average yield if grown using this technique, and also fares particularly well in both hydroponic and aeroponic grows. To get the best out of her in those situations, switch clones or seedlings directly to a 12 on/12 off light cycle, as giving a vegetation period can allow the plants to grow totally out of control. The flowering cycle is fairly short, thanks to the influence of the Bilbao cut, and if grown outdoors, one plant can give up to a kilogram of dried bud – which is a huge harvest by anyone's standards. If this strain is as addictive as its namesake, you'll want to keep a mother plant to clone from, and you're in luck; if you keep a mother plant healthy then she'll give you clones forever.

Dr. Underground, Spain

Sativa-Dominant

Genetics: Destroyer x Critical +

Potency: THC 17%

drunderground.com

As you might expect from the name, this strain is pretty serious shit. Just a few tokes of Crystal M.E.T.H. takes you straight out of reality and dumps you in a higher level of understanding. Just be sure to know when to put down the bong and get back to real life.

haze

...s have been producing fantastic strains over the last decade and their Delahaze strain is a mostly-sativa cross of Haze, which is known for its potency and its exhilarating high. This cross maintains that trait and also gives a great yield, making this a very worthwhile plant to grow!

These plants branch out well and do so early, with many bud sites, so the breeders also recommend that you induce flowering before they get too large. Unlike many sativa-dominant strains, Delahaze finishes in about 9 weeks, although the breeders recommend that you leave the crop one extra week where possible, as this will bring out the mango and citrus aromas and will give you the heaviest harvest. If growing outdoors, look to finish around the start of November, when you should be able to get a colossal yield of around 2.2 pounds per plant, if you can believe it! Indoors the yield is slightly lighter, at around 500 grams per square yard of grow room.

The fruity but Haze-y smoke will give way to a definite creeper of a high, which is crystal clear and incredibly uplifting. With no psychedelic effects this is a totally stimulating feeling that makes you feel like you can walk to Mexico and back without even breaking a sweat. Beware of actually trying to do so, as you might have troubles getting back over the border.

Paradise Seeds, Holland

Sativa-Dominant

Genetics: Unknown

Haze cross

Potency: THC 15-18%

paradise-seeds.com

Denver Diesel

There's nothing like a bit of love for your hometown, and Colorado's Karmaceuticals have certainly pleased the pot smokers of Denver by naming their fantastic Diesel strain after their hometown. A mix of Karma Diesel with Double Diesel, Denver Diesel is a heavy sativa-dominant strain created in 2010 that's perfect for more experienced growers looking to grow something beyond the norm.

As seeds are not yet commercially available, these bad boys can only be grown from clones – though clones have a better success rate than seeds, so this is no bad thing. Denver Diesel can be grown either indoors or outdoors, but it enjoys a colder climate than its Californian cousins so be sure to keep the plants indoors with a controlled atmosphere if you live in a hotter area. These plants won't get beyond 5 feet in height as long as you keep them close to the lights (but not close enough to get burned) and the flowering time sits around 60 days. You should plan your harvest for 50 days after forced flowering.

Karmaceuticals LLC,
USA
Sativa-Dominant
Genetics: Karma Diesel x
Double Diesel
Potency: THC 18%
facebook.com/
karmaceuticals

Denver Diesel will give you the good ol' munchies pretty bad. The smoke leaves you highly alert and hungry, like a coyote prowling for food, although you'll be much more social than a coyote, and incidents of Denver Diesel-induced biting are minimal, as far as I know.

Diabolic Funxta

Many breeders these days advocate wholly organic grow operations, and Don't Panic Organix is at the forefront of this movement. Breeder Eddie Funxta grows only organically and is passionate about preserving the health and taste of his plants this way, especially as he grows predominantly for medical patients – and with such genetically rich plants, it's easy to see why he'd want to take care of them. Diabolic Funxta is a true American strain, a cross between a Sour Diesel plant from the East Coast of the U.S. and the breeder's own American Funxta, which itself is a backcrossed Platinum OG Kush plant. If this doesn't have you singing "The Star Spangled Banner" by the time you've smoked a bowl, then nothing will.

Indoor growers may expect that this strain will be unsuitable for them, as its heavy sativa dominance will bring about tall plants, but when grown inside plants can be kept under 6 feet with careful cultivation. Their true home, though, is outdoors or in a greenhouse, where the extra room to spread will allow for optimum growth, and, therefore, enhanced yields because these plants can grow as tall as 12 feet. With extra room plants will bloom out into beautiful shapes with many branches, which will benefit from having fans directed onto them if you're growing indoors; the movement of the air mimics the wind, and encourages the branches to grow stronger. In a natural outdoor scenario, this strain will take a full 24 weeks from seed to harvest, though shorter times can be had indoors with forced flowering. Though the breeder strongly recommends growing in soil, and starting with large pots to allow for root growth, these plants will also tolerate a hydroponic set up, and in fact will finish earlier in a hydro grow. Either way, your resulting buds will be well worth the extended grow period, not just because of their ravishing good looks.

Don't Panic Organix, USA

Sativa-Dominant

Genetics: East Coast Sour Diesel x American Funxta

Potency: THC 18%

dontpanicorganix.com

Once cured, your harvested buds will remind you of their Sour Diesel parentage with their aroma of fuel and citrus fruits. The smoke also combines a fresh, flowery taste, and is a bit of a cougher. It has been noted to work well for those suffering from directed pain, with affected areas like the back and head, and is great for alleviating pressure behind the eyes and chronic pain in the neck. It can also be of great help to those with autoimmune diseases or diseases that attack the cells. Of course, no strain is purely a medical strain, and recreational users will find that Diabolic Funxta is anything but devilish, bringing on a gorgeously positive head high that gives the body a buzz, too.

Disease Haze

Named after something you might get after a bad bout of typhoid in the Amazonian jungle, Disease Haze from Ultimate Seeds is in fact a result of two amazing Amnesia Haze cuts, and though it will give you a heavy dose of confusion and possibly hallucinations, this is due to it being a kickass sativa strain and isn't anything to do with the dehydration you suffer after pooping yourself all day long.

Parent plant Amnesia Haze is known for being a brilliant expression of the sativa form, and Disease Haze shares this gorgeous sativa structure with its momma. Some training or cropping will be necessary if you plan to grow indoors, but it won't get as large as some pure sativas can. It can grow leggy if the lights are kept too far from the seedlings in the vegetative stage, so be sure to treat the babies with extra care and you'll be rewarded later on. With lots of light and feeding, this strain can be a heavy yielder, and at the end of the 12-week flowering stage your plants will be dripping with giant trichomes on everything but the stems.

Ultimate Seeds

Sativa-Dominant

Genetics: Amnesia Haze x Amnesia Haze

Potency: THC 23%

ultimateseeds.com

They don't call the parents Amnesia Haze for nothing: this strain will take your memory and put it on backwards. Just one hit is enough to get you stoned, and if you keep on tokin', you'll find yourself unable to remember your own name, let alone where you put the pipe down.

Doby

Working out of the U.S., Sativa Tim is a passionate private breeder whose love for this amazing plant is second to none. His main aim is to create strains that give relief for medical problems. Doby is a three-way cross between an Apollo 11 a Green Giant from the Brothers Grimm and an Asia Girl from Reeferman Seeds.

Doby is a great plant for all levels of grow expertise, from the novice to the expert, and is a great choice if you're an indoor grower who is looking to find a workable sativa strain. This strain will only grow to 3.5 feet, and you'll see fantastic vigor in almost any system, but she does enjoy a fairly simple nutrient regimen. As for watering, the breeder recommends always letting the top inch of soil dry out before watering to keep this strain at its best. One of the most notable of Doby's features is her resistance to pests; even kept in a room infected by both thrips and spider mites she manages to stay mostly pest-free. Impressive, no?

You can expect to harvest about 125 grams per Doby plant, and these will be gorgeous little leafless nugs that make manicuring a dream. The high, too, is very dreamy: heady and happy without being too deep. I like to think of this strain as almost-namesake Dobby from UK sitcom Peep Show: lovable and a little odd, but strangely attractive and a lot of fun.

PHOTOS BY RYKA IMAGING

Sativa Tim, USA

Sativa-Dominant

Genetics: Apollo 11 x

Asia Girl x Green Giant

facebook.com/people/

sativa-tim

Dready Cheese

Working out of the UK, Dready Seeds produce very distinctive varieties of well-known strains, and this, their variation on the Cheese family, is no different. Crossing an Original UK Cheese female plant with a male Skunk #1 plant, the Dready guys have come up with an original strain that is notable in its own right.

Backcrossed over several generations to ensure optimum stability, Dready Cheese grows well in all situations but does need consistent temperatures, so any significant drop during the dark period can bring on unwanted deficiencies as well as those gorgeous purple colorings. As the branches tend to grow quite long, it will need good support, and netting will maximize the yield. Towards the end of the flowering stage a carbon filter will be absolutely essential indoors, otherwise you'll stink out not just the grow room but about the whole block, and that just isn't very inconspicuous.

Depending on how carried away you get, your experiences with Dready Cheese be vastly different. At lower doses this strain gives a very cerebral and uplifting high, but at higher doses it becomes more like an indica smoke. If it's a wake and bake you're after, just enjoy a small joint, or you might go all zombie on the bus and find yourself eight miles from where you actually meant to be – both physically and mentally.

Dready Seeds, UK

Sativa-Dominant

Genetics: Original UK Cheese x Skunk #1

Potency: THC 15-20%

dreadyseeds.com

Durban Poison

Weed.co.za is a fantastic online forum dedicated to spreading the word about marijuana strains in their native South Africa. Much like Australia and New Zealand, South Africa is too often overlooked by the North American cannabis community, which is criminal, as there are a whole host of amazing landrace strains that grow beautifully in that area. Durban Poison is one of the more well known of these, hailing from the Durban region, and though it was popularized in the 70s it still remains the favorite of many to this very day.

Durban Poison makes a wonderful choice for breeding stock, as its wild nature means its genes can be inconsistent from one plant to the next, bringing great variation from which you can select the best phenotypes and then go on to stabilize them; it's the strain that keeps on giving, if you will. As you might expect from a South African plant, it grows best in hotter climates, though it can also be grown in Europe and North America, and can grow as tall as 12 feet outdoors in optimum conditions. Because of this height, and the feral nature of the plant, this is a strain that is better suited to growers with some experience of growing outdoors and the challenges that come with it. Not everyone can manage such a monster of a plant and may find themselves with more Durban Poison than they can take care of! Plants will be fairly leggy, too, and covered with razor-thin leaves. Of course, there is a large payoff when harvest rolls around, with yields of 500 grams per plant not being unusual. The breeders recommend that you treat your harvested buds to a long curing process in order to bring out the best of the taste and the high.

Weed.co.za, South Africa

Pure Sativa

Genetics: Landrace Durban South African

Potency: THC 10%

weed.co.za

ganja.co.za

In South Africa, Durban Poison buds are made into 'sticks,' which are made by rolling the dried weed in brown paper almost the size of a banana. This is also known as a pencil and can be thought of as some sort of super blunt, which must look like some sort of optical illusion when you see one being smoked. They must be pretty hardcore tokers over there because I'm pretty sure a pencil of this strain would have me squirming around on the floor like a piglet with no arms. The taste might be reminiscent of tobacco but the high definitely is not, with the mad soaring kick taking you off almost instantly. Thankfully your mouth will be too dry to talk much, because you'll be desperate to jabber on like the village idiot for a good few hours. Remember: 'Tis better to be thought a fool and keep silent than open your mouth and remove all doubt.

Dutch Haze

Dutch Passion has been in operation for over twenty years now and has one of the best reputations in the business, and deservedly so. They were one of the first Amsterdam-based seed companies and certainly the one with the most longevity, which surely says more about the quality of their original strains than I ever could. This one, known as Dutch Haze, just in case you're in any confusion about where this company is from, is their answer to many requests for a true Haze strain that delivers great yields with shorter flowering times. To achieve this, their breeders bred a pure Haze plant with their best indica, shortening not only the flowering time but the height of the plant, too, making this a strain that can be grown indoors or outdoors with no problem at all – which should be good news for all those Dutch Passion fans whose prayers have been answered.

Dutch Haze seeds tend to germinate in around 2 days, at which point they should be carefully transplanted into their first pots. They tend to be resistant to both mold and spider mites, though you should of course always check for both. A short vegetative stage of 3 weeks will keep the plants fairly compact without compromising the weight of the eventual harvest too much. With this timing, plants will grow to about 4 or 5 feet at the very most, which should be small enough for most indoor set ups and greenhouses, too. However, it should be noted that while these plants start out looking very much likes indicas, their sativa traits will be exposed later in their grow so a considerable amount of stretch can occur in the first few weeks of flowering. To prepare for this, plant any stakes or netting at the start of the vegetative period, or it can be too late by the time they flower. Make sure that your lights are not too far away from the tips of the plants, or they will stretch even further to reach the light. After 30 days in the flowering period, no more stretching should happen. At the end of flowering, after around 11 weeks, the top colas especially should enjoy a very high calyx-to-leaf ratio, and all the buds will be covered in resin, so much so that looking at your crop is like looking at a field of Christmas trees, all covered in tinsel.

Dutch Passion, Holland
Sativa-Dominant
Genetics: Unknown Haze
x Unknown Indica
Potency: THC 18%
dutch-passion.nl

Haze is one of the most popular types of sativa, and this popularity has a lot to do with the type of high that this strain gives, which is almost beyond words. A soaring, exhilaratingly cerebral rush of energy takes hold and doesn't let up, leaving you almost literally walking on air. My words don't do it justice – you'll have to toke for yourselves.

PHOTOS BY GBI

Eclipse

With a coffeeshop in Amsterdam as well as a seed company, Homegrown Fantaseeds definitely know the marijuana industry, and the quality of their seeds shows that they are serious breeders, too. They're not afraid to make genetic pairings that go a little beyond the norm, and give fun hybrids that are a little different, and this makes them indispensible in the cannabis community. For this strain, they've taken a Bubble Gum cut from '95 and a twelfth generation Hindu Kush plant to create an incredibly fruity and flavorful sativa-dominant hybrid that appeals to anyone with a sweet tooth.

Eclipse is a 60/40 sativa-indica mix, so these plants look very indica-like in their structure while still retaining those sativa growth patterns. This makes the plant a great choice for any home grower, especially one who wants to grow a sativa-dominant but for whom space is an issue. A SOG set up can help to really get the best out of this plant, and manage the growth while still getting the most bud for your buck. Eclipse also thrives in hydroponics set ups, and can be an absolute beauty in

Homegrown Fantaseeds,
Holland
Sativa-Dominant
Genetics: Bubble Gum
95 x Hindu Kush #12
Potency: THC 17%
homegrown-fan-
taseeds.com

organic soil grows, but she needs a solid 8 weeks of growth before she's ready to harvest. You can extend this to 10 weeks if you so wish, but any longer than this is somewhat pointless as resin production peaks in the 8th week. This strain is an especially stinky one when it reaches maturity so proper filtering, with carbon filters where possible, is going to be a necessity unless you want all your neighbors knocking on the door hoping to smoke a bowl with you.

The Bubble Gum taste comes straight through when you take your first toke of Eclipse, and it's so sweet and bubbly that it's a very addictive smoke. Usually, sugary buds are something to avoid as it means the dealer has rolled the nugs in sugar to increase their weight, but don't go starting any fights this time; they're meant to be so sweet! The high, too, is very energetic: a cerebral, ecstatic feeling with slight psychoactive tendencies. This is probably due to the Hindu Kush plant, and you'll be glad of the mind-expanding properties of the more mature parent plant as they'll stop you from reverting completely back into your six-year-old self and embarrassing everyone by having a temper tantrum if other people take too long with the joint. Even with the Kush influence, the whole experience will leave you feeling like a child again: mouth full of bubble gum, giggling away on the sofa until you exhaust yourself, run out of breath and fall asleep where you're sitting.

Erdbeer (Original Swiss Strawberry)

Alpine Seeds have gained themselves a reputation for fantastic niche strains which are highly stabilized. Erdbeer, which is German for Strawberry, is revered as a fantastic outdoor strain and is regarded as one of the best Swiss strains available. Though the genetics are somewhat unknown, it is a sativa-dominant and likely has some Afghani influence in there.

The breeders at Alpine Seeds have backcrossed their original Strawberry clones

Alpine Seeds, Spain

Sativa-Dominant

Genetics: Original Swiss Strawberry

Potency: THC 18%

alpine-seeds.net

to stabilize this plant and as such, it is a very reliable one to grow, giving fantastically uniform crops. While Erdbeer can grow well in an indoor set up, it will not reach its full potential as it does under natural light and with more space to spread. It's high resistance to mold means it can withstand the changing temperatures and humidity without its dense nugs suffering damage.

The dried buds of an Erdbeer plant give a summer fruit taste and can be very potent, though it can be difficult to pace yourself when the flavors are as good as this! The high is a very active, creative one but creeps in with some Afghani body effects, too.

Fuma Con Dios

Flying Dutchmen have been working out of Holland for almost fifteen years now, and in that time have enjoyed widespread acclaim for their use of "true breeding" strains as the basis for their original varieties. Their Fuma Con Dios strain, the name of which is Spanish for "Smoke with God," is a crossbreed of a pure Haze plant from the 70s with a Skunk F1, a plant that would surely fetch a high price in anyone's mind. Such rare and quality genetic building blocks could not fail to produce a phenomenal plant, and as such, Fuma Con Dios might just fulfill the promise that its name makes.

Fuma Con Dios seeds are always light rather than dark and enjoy a high rate of germination – so be wary if you receive darker seeds that are slow to germinate, as they might not be true seeds of this strain. This F1 hybrid plant has dominant sativa genes, and as such grows with a typical sativa appearance right from the get-go. If growing from clone, which is often a more successful and reliable way of starting a plant than growing from seeds, you can put your little ladies into a 12 on/12 off flowering cycle almost immediately. Of course, this can only happen if you have a source of clones, so research the dispensaries in your area and you might get lucky. The indica genetics present in the Skunk father mean that Fuma Con Dios plants will only reach around 6 feet in height, making them perfect for greenhouse cultivation or outdoor crops. This same set of genes allows the plant to fully flower in 12 weeks. Commercial growers will love this particular trait, as pure Haze plants are often too much work and take too long to be worthwhile for them; with Fuma Con Dios, they can regularly harvest large amounts of a Haze derivative strain, and can get on with shifting that to their Haze-hungry customers instead of camping out for weeks on end to make sure their precious ladies aren't being found. This amount of caution would be totally justified; by the end of flowering these plants will be absolutely covered in bud sites, with the whole top of the plant swimming in pointed, lengthy and delicious looking buds.

Flying Dutchmen,
Holland
Sativa-Dominant
Genetics: Haze x Skunk F1
Potency: THC 16%
flyingdutchmen.com

The harvested nugs, once dried, will show their indica influence in their density and their attractiveness. The smoke is smooth and clear, with a fruity taste with a sharp sweetness that is 100% Haze, as you would expect from a strain so close to the original 70s Haze plant. The complex taste and smell could leave you pondering for hours if your brain didn't take off running within a few seconds of toking and refuse to stop for hours. Best to just let it go, I think.

Grapefruit

Female Seeds, based in the Netherlands, are one of a growing number of seed companies offering only feminized seeds in order to make home growing easier for customers worldwide. By using feminized seeds, you don't have to worry about male plants cropping up and pollinating your unsuspecting and valuable female plants, so obviously these kinds of seeds have become very popular among newer growers. Grapefruit was borne of an auto-flowering sativa plant, which is relatively rare, and the much loved Cindy 99 strain from the Brothers Grimm. Cindy 99, often described as the "Holy Grail" of cannabis plants, came from a process of backcrossing an incredible Princess strain, which was itself a product of a Jack Herer plant and a Haze plant. The result is a hybrid which is 75% Cindy 99 and 25% fruity sativa, the latter of which gives the strain the grapefruit flavor from which it gets its name.

As Grapefruit has only one auto-flowering parent strain, she is only semi-auto-flowering, which means she'll flower under 24 hours in low light conditions. This is no negative trait, though, and indeed Grapefruit plants have been popular for years. Grapefruit seeds tend to germinate between 24 and 48 hours after they've been placed between sheets of wet paper towel, and they can then be transplanted into 2-gallon pots as seedlings. As you get further into the vegetative stage you'll note that your crop is very uniform, with plants being similar in both height and node spacing. It's also interesting to note that she carries many traits of the old school landrace sativas, except that while you could actually grow old waiting for those bad girls to mature, Grapefruit finishes flowering in just 8 weeks – a very fast turnaround time for a sativa-dominant plant. The phenotype of this generation's Grapefruit was selected for shorter plants, so indoor plants should not reach beyond 2 feet, bringing all the benefits of an indica stature to a sativa plant.

Female Seeds, Holland

Sativa-Dominant

Genetics: Cindy 99 x Auto-Flowering Sativa

Potency: THC 17%

femaleseeds.nl

There can be no confusion as to why Grapefruit buds are so called; even before they're burned, the buds give off the gorgeous smell of perfectly ripe grapefruit and will have you dreaming of hot summer days when there can be no better breakfast than that. Once you've brought yourself out of that daydream and taken your first bong hit, the intensely flavorful taste and tropical, clear high will kick in and have you giggling like a madman. The effects are very much sativa-based, and this strain gives you a heap of energy that you'll have to get out by wakeboarding or ballroom dancing or whatever activity floats your boat; just be sure to keep moving to harness that fantastic vivacity!

Grapefruit Fly

Mosca Seeds are a relatively new seed company producing great strains made from the finest American genetics. This Grapefruit Fly strain results from the union of a Special Grapefruit mamma, originally from Reeferman, with a Cinderella 99 male that has proven itself to be great breeding stock.

Grapefruit Fly grows very rapidly and forms a structure that is much stronger than the average sativa, and so is normally able to hold its own branches without support until the end of the flowering period, at which point you might find that staking will help. The huge amounts of solid buds form very dense colas, especially if you use high intensity lighting in your grow room. Despite being such a great producer, this strain is also an easy one to cultivate, and you'll enjoy a fantastic aroma for a few weeks before harvest. Expect a flowering period of 60 days, after which you'll be astounded by the lime-colored buds and their excellent bag appeal. This strain is on limited release so don't miss out!

PHOTOS BY ICETOKER

Mosca Seeds, USA

Sativa-Dominant

Genetics: Grapefruit x

Cinderella 99

Potency: THC 17%

seedsman.com

The aroma of these cured buds is Sweet Pink Grapefruit through and through, and the effects are just as refreshing. You'll feel a rush to your head that spreads to your body, and then you'll barely be able to keep yourself still. Definitely one that leaves you flying!

Green Crack

Also known as Cush, Green Goblin and Green Candy, – which is, of course, why we're big fans of it – Green Crack is a Clone Only strain that originated in Athens, of all places, back in the early 90s. It was randomly created by breeder CecilC and was distributed by Mrgreenbeans in 1994. SinsemillaWorks! have been growing the real Green Crack for years and now sell clones to keep this gorgeous plant thriving in the scene.

A 75% sativa strain, Green Crack can be grown indoors at a height of between 3 and 6 feet, and is suitable for ScrOG growing. It can do well in both hydro and organic soil set ups, but for either type of grow, the room temperature should be set between 78 and 88 Fahrenheit with a humidity of 45 to 55%. It is also recommended that you top her 2 weeks before you switch her to a 12 on/12 off light cycle and 'lollipop' her one week after that. She doesn't need to be excessively fed, and in fact during the first 3 weeks of growth she should only be sprayed with reverse osmosis water once a day. After forced flowering, the buds should show hints of pink and blue and will be fully finished in 45 days.

PHOTOS BY GIORGIO ALVAREZZO

SinsemillaWorks!, USA

Sativa-Dominant

Genetics: 1980 SSSC M39 Skunk #1 x (Blue Cheese x Korean Skunk)

Potency: THC 15%

facebook.com/SinsemillaWorks

This is the perfect summer smoke, as it tastes of super ripe mangoes and melts into a very creative, mentally active high that's likely to leave you bounding around in the sun like a springer spaniel on the happy juice. And who doesn't want that?

Green House Thai

One of the most well-branded seed companies in the world, Green House are like that kid in school who manages to be both popular and attractive while getting fantastic grades, and looks like he's having ridiculous amounts of fun doing so. Not only does this company party with Snoop Dogg and Woody Harrelson, they also drop a pioneering bomb once in a while, like the introduction of their color-coded seeds. If only they weren't so damn likeable!

This Green House Thai plant is, as you'd expect, an exotic mix of Southeast Asian genetics, with its parents coming from Thailand and neighboring Laos. These countries form a veritable hotbed of fantastic sativa genes, and many breeders have made pilgrimages over there in the last couple of decades to find and take home some immense breeding stock. Green House, of course, did not miss the boat.

When considering a Green House Thai crop, it's best to first assess how much space you can allow for each plant. These ladies are very tall, surpassing 7 feet with ease, and most indoor growers may not have the type of

Green House Seed Co., Holland

Sativa-Dominant

Genetics: Thai x Laos

Potency: THC 17.7%

greenhouseseeds.nl

room that can house such huge plants. Though the plants can be tamed somewhat with training, topping and differing techniques, they would be much, much happier outside with plenty of space and plenty of natural sunlight. If you do decide to grow these inside, however, remember that topping will increase bud sites and more bud sites means a great yield. When grown outdoors, this strain is somewhat resistant to colder temperatures and would certainly endure a milder climate, but if growing in the north of America or Canada, or climates similar to those, be aware that the plant should be finished at the start of December. Any longer and the plants will suffer as the frost hits, and you'll risk wasting all your hard work. This is a strain that likes to take its time, and will enjoy a good 15 weeks to properly ripen, but as the old saying goes, "good things come to those who wait". A harvest of 60 grams per square foot is to be expected, or 800 grams per outdoor plant.

Like many other plants from such tropical shores as this one, Green House Thai brings about a very introspective and all-consuming high. Such a heady effect can manifest itself in psychoactive traits or in electric bursts of creativity. Of course, the strength of the high depends on how much you smoke, so if you're down for something approaching an ayahuasca high, then fill your boots, but if you'd just like a kick start in your writing or painting, stick to just a couple of bowls.

Guanabana

Spain's Blim Burn Seeds is a relatively new company, founded by growers with fifteen years' experience in the scene, and the breeders there believe that seeds are a better way to start new plants than working with a cutting from an old plant, as long as the seeds are of very high quality. They aim to produce highly stable strains that have psychoactive qualities. Their Guanabana strain is a particularly strong cerebral plant that comes from the powerful Amnesia Haze, crossed with a Widow plant. Amnesia Haze encompasses Hawaiian, Asian and Jamaican traits and is known to give a very strong heady high – and its offspring is no different!

Despite being more sativa than indica, this strain is recommended for indoor growth, but it is also suitable for outdoor cultivation, and can be harvested in the Northern Hemisphere in late September. The resulting buds are intensely compact and very resinous, and give off a very intense aroma. The breeders recommend, if growing indoors, that the plants be put to flower straight from germination, as this will avoid any problems with the plant growing too large for your compact space. In the flowering stage the buds grow extremely quickly, so it is important to check the flowers on a regular basis, and ensure that the humidity in your grow room doesn't reach beyond acceptable levels. If the humidity gets too high, rapidly growing buds can become susceptible to mold, and your gorgeous nugs will be slowly ruined from the inside. The good news is that Guanabana is highly resistant to botrytis, so you can worry less about that and more about sustaining the best conditions in which your ladies will flourish. Indoors, she'll finish in about 50 days, which is great news for any grower looking for a consistent and fast-finishing crop.

Blim Burn Seeds, Spain

Sativa-Dominant

Genetics: Amnesia Haze x Widow

Potency: THC 17%

blimburnseeds.com

If Guanabana doesn't look like a sativa-dominant plant, she certainly smokes like it. The taste, which gives this strain its name, is very fruity with a sour tang; imagine a mix of strawberry and pineapple with a hint of apple and you're just about there. When you've almost finished pondering over the flavors, your brain will feel the hit of the high, and you'll be riddled with an infectious energy. Anyone who's been lucky enough to smoke Amnesia Haze before will recognize the pulsating feeling in the head and back that lingers pleasantly and leaves you feeling like you've just had an intense massage – but without having to spend $100 bucks or get naked...unless you really want to.

High Level

Spain's Eva Female Seeds are a popular seed company who specialize in producing feminized seeds of their fantastic original strains. One of these aforementioned strains is High Level, a fascinating and unique mix of some very different genetics. One parent plant was a cross of Skunk, the Brad Pitt of the strain world, and Haze, everyone's favorite sativa, while the other parent was an interesting African sativa landrace plant from Lesotho, in South Africa.

Thanks to the landrace influence this is a great choice for an outdoor grow, especially when planted in a straight-up soil set up. As always, you should check the quality of your local soil before you plant, and amend it as necessary to ensure the best quality base for your plants; do a bit of research on potential additives such as perlite, blood meal and sand and your plants will thank you for it. High Level does not easily fall prey to pests, and has a very high resistance to mold, which is good news if you're growing outdoors in a warmer climate. Whether you're growing indoors or outdoors, these plants require plenty of feeding, and once you've flipped them into the flowering period they'll be ravenous; don't leave them hungry and you'll be rewarded with increased growth and, of course, increased yields. If you're not feeding enough, the leaves will drop and your plants will look sad, so watch out for a depressed-looking crop. For the purest sativa-type high available from this strain, the breeders recommend that you harvest when the hairs have mostly turned white, which should be after 8 weeks of bloom. If your High Level crop is outdoors, be ready to harvest in the middle of October. The yield is average to good, but with this strain, quality not quantity is the main focus and when you've cured your buds and smoked it for the first time, you'll see that that dedication to quality has definitely paid off.

Eva Female Seeds, Spain

Sativa-Dominant

Genetics: African Lesotho x (Skunk x Haze)

Potency: THC 17%

evaseeds.com

If you've got a few friends who consider themselves to be the Kings of Cannabis and complain because the old killer strains like Herijuana just don't get them high anymore, you might want to share a few bong hits of this sweet-smelling bud with them; they'll be left wide eyed and very quiet before too long. Behind those glassy eyes their minds will be going wild in a frenzied mess of hyperactivity, and their bodies will soon follow suit too. If you could take a picture of a high (which of course is impossible, unless you've got some sort of metaphysical camera), this one would be next to sativa in the dictionary, as it is all up above the shoulders and could not be more enjoyable.

High Tension

Spain's World of Seeds didn't pick their name out of a hat; the collective is made up of breeders and growers from all over the globe, each bringing their own personal expertise and tricks to the table. With all that knowledge they certainly don't mess around when it comes to creating their own strains, and High Tension is a complex mix of some of the world's best bud. One parent strain is a stabilized blend of Orange Bud, Black Domina from Sensi Seeds and Jack Herer (which is a great combination by anyone's standard), and a Mango Biche plant from Colombia that is out of this world. This plant started life as an Afghani clone which was crossbred with Black Domina and Jack Herer males and so continued its journey to becoming High Tension.

Each of the strains comprised within High Tension has brought its own phenomenal traits to the final plant. Black Domina has brought high tolerance to both irrigation and disease and the Colombian strain has given vigorous growth, while Jack Herer has brought potency and Orange Bud, the amazing flavor. Thanks to such fantastic genetics, High Tension is a great performer both indoors and outdoors, and the resulting buds are both effective and delicious. In growth, these plants can get relatively tall at about 4 feet, and all within 8 weeks. To prevent them from spending any more energy on their height and to force them to concentrate more on flowering, the breeders recommend topping them during the vegetative stage. When she hits the flowering period, you'll be delighted with the tight nugs, and the excellent bud-to-leaf ratio means that she's both good looking and easy to manicure. Harvest should take place at about 9 weeks, but you'll know when the buds are dying to be chopped, as they'll have already turned orange and will be absolutely covered with fat crystals that look like white sugar.

World of Seeds, Spain

Sativa-Dominant

Genetics: Colombian Mango Biche x (Orange Bud x Black Domina x Jack Herer)

Potency: THC 15-20%

worldofseeds.eu

If the influence of all the rest of the family comes out in the growth patterns, the influence of the Jack Herer grandparent strain becomes obvious when you smoke up your first High Tension nug. The strong narcotic effects take you out like William Perry (who you might know better as The Refrigerator), but the high is a surprisingly "up" one after this: you might be laid out with a few bewildered brain cells but your mind will be active and alert. Once you've recovered from the hit you'll be full of vim and spunk and other outdated words, and you don't have to worry about the broken ribs until you wake up the next morning.

Inferno Haze

Gage Green Genetics have recently released the first strain in their Private Collection series; a range of extra-special plants with fantastic traits. Inferno Haze is the first one of these, and is a cross between a clone-only Fire OG Kush mother and an Afghan Haze father, making it a sativa-leaning hybrid with a lot of Haze influence and some of California's best genetics.

This plant's Afghan Haze father is a vigorous and distinctive plant that brings some speed to this F1 cross. As with any F1, there are a number of different phenotypes that may be expressed, the best of which yields very large, very dense buds and has an aroma of just-made candy. Though some phenotypes lean more towards the sativa side and others are more indica, none of these plants should grow excessively tall and all of them will need careful monitoring during the grow period. Orange and white shades should be visible on the buds when the harvest time rolls around, after 8 or 9 weeks. For all phenotypes the yield will be large, and if you're lucky enough to get one of the best, your harvest will be massive.

Gage Green Genetics, USA

Sativa-Dominant

Genetics: Fire OG Kush x Afghan Haze

Potency: THC 21.3%

gagegreen.org

The smoke of Inferno Haze will be a great experience; tasty, aromatic and very uplifting. Even the more indica-leaning phenotypes give a mostly heady high that makes the gamble of the grow very worthwhile.

Island Sweet Skunk

Canada's Next Generation Seed Company started producing unique genetics in the late 90s, and since then have not only given the cannabis world some fantastic strains but have garnered a reputation to match. They consistently perfect their strains and work hard at stabilizing them as much as possible. Most of their genetics come from Canada and the Pacific Northwest and as such, can be great for outdoor grows in North America as well as abroad. For Island Sweet Skunk, they've taken one of the most famous contemporary strains, Skunk, and bred this with a fantastically fruity Grapefruit indica.

Unless you have a particularly high-ceilinged grow room, Island Sweet Skunk can only really be grown outdoors, as it gets to be very tall and as such, won't do well in the confines of a tiny set up. If you do choose to grow outside, and you happen to be located in California or Spain, you'll find that this plant absolutely loves your local climate and will bask in the regular sunshine like a woman of leisure. In such an environment she flourishes and gives an incredibly heavy yield with very long buds. The weight of these nugs will lie heavy on her branches, so you'll almost definitely have to assist her in the later stages by staking and supporting some of the weight. If you do have the room to satisfy these ladies inside, then you can expect a flowering time of 65 days, whereas outdoor growers will be looking to harvest between October 15th and 25th in the Northern hemisphere. If you live in British Columbia, you will have to grow inside, as this strain can't handle the excessive cold. A plain soil grow with minimal nutrients will be more than enough for these plants, though they can be raised in a SOG system in which they will not need to be given a vegetation period; this will keep them small enough to work with, otherwise come harvest time you'll be wrestling with a giant spider-like structure and you will not win.

Next Generation Seed Company, Canada

Sativa-Dominant

Genetics: Skunk x Grapefruit Indica

Potency: THC 17%

greenlifeseeds.com

If you think Island Sweet Skunk buds smell tasty when they're growing, then sit down for your first whiff after the curing period as it will knock your head off. The taste is a perfect balance of that Skunky sweetness that everyone loves and the tangy fruitiness of the Grapefruit parent. The high is no less amazing, creeping into your brain then right down into your whole body. It's amazing that boxers looking to drop a weight class don't turn to Island Sweet Skunk as it makes you sweat like a madman in the high of a Hawaiian summer. Surely that's got to be more fun than running in those weird suit things?

Jack Flash

If you've not heard of Sensi Seeds, then you definitely don't live in or around the Netherlands, where this company has been working for over 25 years and where they even have their own official stamp – which is quite a testament to the impact these guys have made. This is thanks to both the quality of the strains and their resolve to improve upon their own work again and again, and it's this resolve that has given rise to the Jack Flash seed-strain and its feminized counterpart, Jack Flash #5.

As the first stable hybrid bred from the Jack Herer line, the original Jack Flash was created by back-crossing a Jack Herer mother with a blend of Super Skunk and Haze in order to stabilize and refine the most desired traits of all three strains. Jack Flash #5 is the all-female version, which was carefully bred in order to keep it as close as possible to the original throughout the feminizing process, Both versions of Jack Flash seeds produce plants which are hugely potent, reliable and consistent to grow.

The four phenotypes of Jack Herer have been narrowed down to two in Jack Flash, one more indica in growth and one more sativa. The indica phenotype is more compact in structure, and is the better choice for indoor and greenhouse growing. During flowering you'll see rapid and uniform bud development, with the calyxes even sitting on top of each other to form rope-like links. The sativa phenotype, on the other hand, expresses itself in a large form plant that gains even more height in the flowering stage. The breeders recommend that the sativa-like form is allowed to grow up to 4 feet or beyond, as the structure fills out totally with large buds in the final stages. Jack Flash #5 tends to produce a higher proportion of sativa phenotypes than regular Jack Flash.

Sensi Seeds, Holland

Sativa-Dominant

Genetics: Jack Herer x (Super Skunk x Haze)

Potency: THC 19%

sensiseeds.com

When growing this strain outside, care should be taken to keep pests at bay, as it can be difficult when dealing with such large plants to check them thoroughly for any signs of an infestation. With such large nugs too, if growing the indica phenotype especially, you should take care to ensure that the humidity in your grow room isn't too high. Indoors, this strain finishes in 55 to 75 days, depending on which phenotype you have, and you can expect a yield of up to 125 grams per plant from larger plants.

When you smoke up your first Jack Flash blunt you'll see why it's gained such a good reputation. It completely does a number on you; smacks a grin right on your face, takes the top off your head and replaces your legs with an unknown substance that is much like jelly, but a bit heavier.

Jack Horror (AKA Jack F1)

Holland's Spliff Seeds are already known for producing high-quality strains, so when they dub their new products as the "Silver Line" of seeds, you know that they're something extra special. Jack Horror is one of these silver strains, and when you look at the family history it's easy to see why they've elevated it to seed royalty. With Northern Lights, an F1 cut of the crazy famous Skunk, and a double dose of Haze genetics comprising the strain, Jack Horror is the cannabis equivalent of the resulting child if Marlon Brando and twin James Deans all had an orgy and simultaneously impregnated Marilyn Monroe. That's got to be worth at least one star on the Amsterdam Walk of Fame.

This amalgamation of phenomenal genetics is the result of years of selective breeding by the guys over at Spliff Seeds. Both the Northern Lights x Haze mother and the Skunk F1 x Haze father are 5th generation, following a labor-intensive process of picking the best phenotypes again and again, so both are very stable and great stock for breeding. Jack Horror is a 90/10 sativa-indica hybrid, and has the combination of traits that make any strain the holy grail for growers: it grows like an indica but smokes like a sativa.

Spliff Seeds, Holland

Sativa-Dominant

Genetics: (Northern Lights x Haze) x (Skunk F1 x Haze)

Potency: THC 20%

spliff.nl

This means that a crop of Jack Horror plants will be shorter and bushier than most sativas, but will give a good amount of bud. When grown inside they'll get up to 6 feet, but outdoors they take on a whole life of their own and grow right up to 10 feet or more, but always with one solid main cola that shouldn't be pruned. The breeders advise that you use a soil grow and don't overfeed, keeping nutrients to a minimum especially in the 4-week vegetative period if you don't want to stunt your plants. Lighting should stay on a 24/7 schedule for best results and by the end of the 9-week flowering period, when the lights are bouncing off her shimmering buds, you'll be glad you didn't put her in the dark.

As the grow is so easy, you might think that the 'Horror' of this strain's name comes in the smoke; but aside from it being a bit of a cougher, there's nothing horrific about it. Rather, the high is an accelerating one in all regards: physically, mentally, and in terms of how quickly you'll get through your stash. Even the taste is beyond the norm, with a combination of sweetness and spiciness that tastes like cinnamon Haze cookies. Like all good sativa-dominants, a Jack Horror high is almost all in the head, with just the right amount of body tingle to form the perfect stone.

Jack O Nesia

If you know anything about sativa, then you've heard of Amnesia. Along with Haze and Diesel, it is one of the most famous of the sativa families and literally dozens of variants of it are commercially available. Jack O Nesia is Karma Genetics' Amnesia variety, bred from a female D-cut of Amnesia and a male plant of Sensi's Jack Herer #22. Both Amnesia and Jack Herer are products of Haze, Northern Lights #5 and Skunk genes, so Jack O Nesia has a family tree more extensive and inbred than the British Royal Family – and just as regal.

This strain is noted as an easy one to grow, as she does not require a lot of feeding and prefers a distilled water feed than one loaded with expensive nutrients. If you want to give her a treat, try feeding with water and molasses, but be sure to switch to plain water again before harvest. The stretch is fairly prominent, meaning that she will produce much more when given lots of space, and she responds especially well to being topped. You'll almost be sad when it's time to harvest around the 12-week mark because she's so lovely to grow!

If you can leave Jack O Nesia buds to cure for at least 4 weeks, you'll be rewarded with a super smooth lemony-diesel smoke that leads into an extremely clear, inspiring head high that leaves you feeling wide awake.

PHOTOS BY OCANABIS

Karma Genetics, Holland; Grown by Ocanabis

Sativa-Dominant

Genetics: Amnesia (D-cut) x Jack #22

Potency: THC 17%

karmagenetics.com

Jazz

Dr. Greenthumb is based in Canada and has been producing high-grade seeds for over fifteen years. Jazz is a product of a Mexican sativa, known as Oaxacan after the region it grows in, and an indica from Iran.

Despite its heritage, Jazz grows best in colder climates, and can be grown either indoors or outdoors without much trouble. Indoors the plants grow between 3 to 4 feet tall, but outdoors can reach 6 feet in the right temperatures. This strain tends to do well in both hydro and soil set ups, and can be a good plant to use in both SOG and ScrOG grows. It should be moved into the flowering stage at around 60 days, and from that point, will be fully mature and begging to be harvested in 63 days. The breeder's suggestion is to force flowering when the plant is 8 inches tall, to end up with a 30-inch finished plant – one that is very manageable but will also give a good yield. She is an easy one to grow, doesn't need any particular feeding or nutrient regime and resists all pests and problems fairly well.

Dr. Greenthumb Seeds, Canada

Sativa-Dominant

Genetics: Oaxacan x Iranian Indica

Potency: THC 17%

drgreenthumb.com

Well-cured Jazz buds will give a peppery, hashy taste with a hint of medicine. The effects are almost entirely in the head with only a slight body buzz, but you won't even be thinking about your body as your mind soars through a trippy, almost narcotic high.

Juanita La Lagrimosa

I'm a big fan of Spain's Reggae Seeds, not only because I listen to the same genre of music as they do (along with every other self-respecting stoner!) but because their strains are always amazing looking. It's some dedication not only to name your company after the music you love, but to make your plants express the colors of that music too – and almost all Reggae Seeds strains express beautiful red, green and yellow colorings that go beyond belief! Beauty isn't the only goal for this company though, and their original strains are as hard-hitting as they are attractive. Juanita La Lagrimosa, which translates as Juanita's Tear, is no different, and with Mexican and Afghani landrace genetics, the high is a special one indeed. These plants were bred into each other and then crossed with Reina Madre, also known as Queen Mother, bringing a whole other regal level of quality to an already fantastic plant.

There's no question that this is a sativa-dominant strain, with the young plants showing that typical sativa growth pattern right from the beginning. It's a good idea to keep an eye on the stalks, as they'll need to be strong for when the flowering period rolls around. Vibrating the stalks between your index and first finger regularly can help strengthen them. Flowering indoors should last around 60 to 65 days, and if you're growing outdoors you can expect to harvest around the first two weeks of October. An indoor grow can give around 500 grams per square yard of grow space when fully finished. As with most sativas, you can get the most bang for your buck if you grow outdoors and let the plant get fairly massive, with the final yield being anywhere from 700 grams to a solid one kilogram per square yard of outdoor grow space. Yep, you can read that part again if you like. This is a relatively easy plant to grow, especially outdoors, and in fact the biggest problem you'll face is likely to be finding somewhere big enough to dry such a massive harvest!

Reggae Seeds, Spain

Sativa-Dominant

Genetics: (Mexican x Afghani) x Reina Madre

Potency: THC 6.77%

reggaeseeds.com

The fully cured buds of Juanita La Lagrimosa are not only a treat to look at but are also a treat to smell; the citrusy, pine scent will leave you drooling from the mouth and weirdly hungry. Try not to eat the buds though; they're much better smoked – and trust me, I've tried both. The resulting experience will be a very, very clear social high that sets your mind on Warp Factor 7 and doesn't stop 'til you're at the other side of a galaxy far, far away. This might sound fantastic, but hitchhiking home is a nightmare. Don't panic, though; just have another bowl. Juanita has everything you need right here.

K-13 Haze

If Nietzsche smoked pot, he would most definitely smoke the stuff from fantastic Spanish company Philosopher Seeds. Not only does their company name do justice to his eternal musings, but he was a huge fan of Spanish moustaches and loved growing things in 3-gallon pots. Marijuana has long been known to bring about original thought and fairly bizarre ramblings (no, really!) but it takes a special strain to make even mad philosophers go over the top. After flicking through this company's brochure Nietzsche would probably choose K-13 Haze, a cross between two fantastic strains: Kali Mist and Yumbolt. Just don't make the pun about his 'hazey' final years. He wouldn't like that at all.

Like any good hybrid, K-13 Haze has inherited the best traits of both its parent plants, namely the compact structure of the Yumbolt and the clear high and aromatic buds of the Kali Mist. Despite being a sativa-dom, this plant is very indica-like in structure, with dense branching and a fairly squat frame. For this reason, it's not the best choice for a SOG system, and instead enjoys soil grows in 3-gallon pots indoors. Outdoors, containers should be up to three times larger to allow for maximum growth and therefore maximum yield. The heavy branching means that it's important, when planting, to give each seedling plenty of room around it, so it's easy to get to all parts of the plant, even when they're fully grown. Anyone who's ever grown a dense plant had made the mistake of planting them all too close to each other, resulting very quickly in an impenetrable jungle of weed that looks and smells great but is an absolute nightmare to get through whenever you want to water them! Avoid this by planning ahead and even, if need be, growing less plants per season if your limited grow space necessitates it. Whatever your grow method, after 50 days of flowering you'll be ready to chop the beautiful, golden colas that should weigh in at about 450 grams per square yard of grow space. Outdoors, harvest can be anywhere from late September to mid-October, depending on your location.

Philosopher Seeds, Spain
Sativa-Dominant
Genetics: Kali Mist x Yumbolt
Potency: THC 16-18%
philosopherseeds.com
alchimiaweb.com

An extended curing period is always great to bring out the best flavors and high of a strain and this one is no different. The effects of this strain are pure Haze: a very cerebral, if somewhat scattered, head high that can both trip you out beyond rationality and bring out some of your most deep-rooted, profound ideas. It's not hard to believe it was the influence of a fat K-13 Haze joint that led our friend Friedrich to claim that God is dead, just before he flicked on *The Big Lebowski* (again) and finished off a Big Gulp.

Kaia Kush (Sativa Hybrid)

Apothecary Genetics is a U.S.-based seed company dedicated to providing good medicine for those who need it. The sativa hybrid of Kaia Kush is a beautiful plant, and is the product of breeding OG Super Silver Haze with a Kush plant. The Super Silver Haze parent is itself an amalgamation of Haze, Skunk and Northern Lights genetics, a list that might have been ripped from the opening page of the Who's Who of cannabis strains, if such a thing existed (by the way, it does – you're holding it).

One of the most notable things about Kaia Kush is its incredibly sturdy stalk and branch structure. The leaves will be a healthy deep green, with black hues coming through in the final stages of life. Later in flowering the buds will grow dense and heavy, but the aforementioned strong structure will allow the plants to hold their own weight without needing much assistance. You'll be too transfixed by the buds to worry about that, though, as this strain exhibits foxtailing traits; the buds appear to be covered in little spikes, or miniature hands throwing the devil horns at an AC/DC gig.

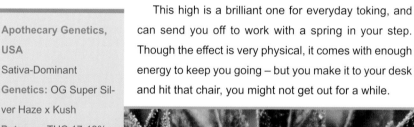

Apothecary Genetics, USA

Sativa-Dominant

Genetics: OG Super Silver Haze x Kush

Potency: THC 17-19%

apothecarygenetics.com

This high is a brilliant one for everyday toking, and can send you off to work with a spring in your step. Though the effect is very physical, it comes with enough energy to keep you going – but you make it to your desk and hit that chair, you might not get out for a while.

Kaligria

The guys at All Star Genetics have been around the Amsterdam cannabis scene since the early 90s, and are always working on new strains to offer to the world. Kaligria is a cross between a Kali Mist male and a clone from an Alegria female. Alegria is well known in Holland for its fabulous taste and smell, and Kali Mist is one of the most talked about sativa strains today, famous for its fluffy nugs as much is its heavy yields.

Kaligria has a 70% sativa influence, which shows itself in the plant's stature; it will grow to 5 or 6 feet, or even beyond, if given the extra root space. As such, it can be a difficult plant to grow indoors but will flourish outdoors if the conditions are right, and it is subjected to a moderate climate like that of northern Europe. The yield is impressive, even more so if grown outside, and the Kali Mist genetics give this plant long colas that can give a harvest of up to 60 grams per square foot. As it matures, the buds will turn light purple with very oily, pink hairs, letting you know around the 9-week mark that it's time to bring in the buds!

ASG Seeds, Holland

Sativa-Dominant

Genetics: Alegria x Kali Mist

Potency: THC 19%

asgseeds.com

Though the buds may have a Skunky smell when growing, the cured Kaligria buds give a deliciously sweet smoke that has quite rightly become a favorite of many Dutch tokers. The high is definitely one that you can feel up top, leaving you energized and satisfied at the same time.

been one of the big names in modern cannabis strains since it first burst onto the scene back in 1992, when Bill Clinton was on his way in and New Kids on the Block were on their way out (thankfully). The guys at Advanced Seeds have obviously seen this strain's stratospheric rise in popularity, and with all the confidence of Icarus, have taken an already great strain and made it even better. By breeding AK-47 with some of their own fantastic genetics, they have created a strain that might even surpass its parent plant. Kaya 47 is a fast flowering, heavier yielding version of AK-47, and the quality of this plant means that for Advanced Seeds, there's definitely not going to be a fall back to Earth.

As this strain is only slightly sativa-dominant, it can be grown in fairly small areas and grow rooms that don't have the space for huge monster plants. She can be grown on a 12 on/12 off light cycle from the very beginning, and on this sort of schedule will be fully finished in just 90 days. The plant will develop a large and dense central cola surrounded by a good amount of secondary buds, creating a fantastic-looking plant that can be kept to very small sizes; I know of one grower who kept the plant to less than one foot tall in a grow inside a PC case. Of course, such small plants will give less bud, but for some, quality is more important than quantity. The ease of growing Kaya 47 makes it an absolutely phenomenal choice for the first time grower, although of course more experienced cultivators will be able to use their own tips and tricks to get even more out of this plant. Cutting back the fan leaves can be a good plan, and a good long flush with black molasses can help bring out the natural flavors of this strain and get rid of any chemical aftertaste that might linger in the finished buds. If you're really going for the ultimate win, team these molasses with organic bee honey and you'll have a smoke that is second to none.

Advanced Seeds, Spain

Sativa-Dominant

Genetics: AK-47

Potency: THC 22%

advancedseeds.com

Much like its parent strain, Kaya 47 is a one-hitter-quitter; all but the most experienced of smokers will only need a toke or two before they're flat on their ass wondering what the hell just happened. The long-lasting effects will leave you well medicated but also mellow, with enough mental activity coming back after a little while to keep you from being totally zombified. Rookie smokers should definitely be wary of getting carried away with this strain, as their virgin lungs are likely to be shocked by the strength of this strain and might run terrified into the woods to hide. You'll be able to coax them back with a little effort, but it's best to take it slow in the first place!

Killing Fields

Sannie's Seeds are based in Holland and enjoy a solid reputation thanks to their great original strains like Killing Fields. A cross of Sannie's The One with their Jack F4 plant, Killing Fields is a product of a long line of quality genetics. The One is the result of a Killa Queen / New York City Diesel cross known as Killian and a Blueberry, and is known most of all for its fantastic shape and its aromas of grape and berry. Jack F4 is Sannie's version of the well-known Jack Herer strain, which shows a lot of Haze influence. With a The One mother and a Jack F4 father Killing Fields is part American, part Dutch, and as such can grow tall but also loves listening to Bruce Springsteen.

Every grower strives to have a grow room full of good-looking plants that are a walk in the park to grow, and Killing Fields gives you plants that hit both these buttons. The leaves in particular grow exactly as sativa leaves should, with thin profiles and an intense bright green color. The structure of the plants, too, is that of the typical sativa Christmas-tree shape, so if any of your neighbors pop round you will definitely need a Brilliant Disguise for your crop if you want to keep it as a Secret Garden. These plants continue to grow for 4 weeks after they've been switched to a 12 on/12 off lighting cycle (maybe because they like Dancing in the Dark), so there is no need to allow them a long vegetative period – and doing so is a Risky Business as it might make them grow too large for your space. It's also been suggested that pumping "Born To Run" into your grow room may encourage your plants to grow taller than the other strains, but there is, as yet, no evidence that this is the case. Without the musical interlude, Killing Fields will be about 8 inches tall at the start of the flowering stage and will usually have grown to about 5 feet just before harvest. With a grow room full of plants of this size, you can expect to have a yield of around 550 grams per square yard of grow space. The biggest yields come from a ScrOG set up using an organic soil medium, so this is the recommended technique by the breeder if you're looking for One Step Up from the regular harvest.

Sannie's Seeds, Holland

Sativa-Dominant

Genetics: Sannie's The One x Sannie's Jack F4

Potency: THC 22%

sanniesshop.com

The fat buds you've harvested will give off a spicy and sweet smell of overripe berries, and the resulting high is a very active, cerebral one that's great for a daytime smoke. After a wake 'n bake your head will almost be blown right off, and walking around high as a kite in the sunshine, you'll definitely feel like you're in your Glory Days.

Krystalica

Spain's Mandala Seeds are dedicated to producing interesting strains that give both a vigorous grow and potent high, and they use the best genetics from all over the world in order to do so. Krystalica is a testament to this dedication, as it comprises genes of two wild landrace plants from two very separate parts of the world: Nepal and Kerala in the south of India. Landrace sativas are phenomenal breeding stock, and as such, Krystalica is certainly a strain that commands some attention, and not just because of its incredible parentage.

Krystalica is a high-yielding, very resistant strain with high resin content, quality buds and amazing vigor. She has a high leaf-to-calyx ratio, with the uppermost buds being almost leafless, enjoys a very high resin content, and is extremely mold resistant, making it a fantastic choice for a greenhouse grow where the temperature and humidity can be high. The side shoots will need support in the later weeks of flowering. This plant can be grown both indoors and outdoors, with the plants only growing to about 4 feet on average, but she is not suitable for outdoor growing in cold, northern climates unless you are growing in a heated greenhouse. The breeders recommend that, for an indoor grow, you use 400 to 600 watts of HPS light per 10 square feet, and from this you can expect to harvest up to 450 grams from the same size area. Be sure not to overcrowd your grow space, though, as this will cause the plants to stretch for light. If cultivating Krystalica outdoors, be aware that cold and overcast conditions will negatively affect growth as she naturally prefers a hotter, sunnier climate – and don't we all? Fertilizers rich in nitrogen should be avoided, as should soil mixes with excessive levels of nitrogen. This strain exhibits heightened resistance to both pests and high temperatures and as such, can be a great choice for growers in more tropical climates who like to grow outdoors.

Mandala Seeds, Spain

Sativa-Dominant

Genetics: Landrace South Indian x Landrace Nepali

Potency: THC 23%

mandalaseeds.com

Less overwhelming than Mandala's Satori strain, which can be too strong for a lot of smokers, Krystalica is a great smoke for people who are ready to wind down after a long day but still want a rush of creativity. This will satisfy even hardened smokers with a high tolerance and can be a great sleep-inducer for those with slightly less experience. This is a great sativa choice for medicinal marijuana users and the pineapple and bubble gum flavors make it a strain that you can easily smoke every day without getting bored!

Laughingman

Though they might sound as if they're from beyond the Iron Curtain, Redstar Farms are actually a group of veterans in California who've formed their own collective to produce quality medicinal marijuana strains. They created Laughingman 3 years ago, taking a fantastic OG Kush plant and a Pre-98 Bubba Kush as their breeding stock.

Laughingman can be grown both indoors and outdoors, although the breeder prefers to grow his crop indoors at a temperature of around 70 degrees Fahrenheit. As the plants get closer to harvest, drop the temperature of your grow room to around 64 degrees for the best results. With a height of about 3 feet it is suitable for both ScrOG and SOG techniques, and is as happy in hydro as it is in soil. However, the breeder does recommend Canna nutrients for this variety, and he waters every other day with tea mixes in between feedings. The plant thrives on more feeding closer to harvest. A breeder's tip is to keep the pH between 5.5 and 6.0 in the vegetative stage and 6.0 and 6.6 in the flowering stage – and take off all the extra branches as it grows up to get better quality pot!

Redstar Farms, USA

Sativa-Dominant

Genetics: OG Kush x Pre-98 Bubba Kush

redstar420.com

This finished bud will be citrusy but sweet, like a lemon drop candy, with a euphoric, soaring high that will make you the life and soul of the party – and the one who's eaten all the chips.

Madd Krush

Genetics Gone Madd is the breeder becoming more and more well known for his amazing-looking indica-dominant plant, Redd Cross, which is a distant relative to the Madd Krush. The seeds from which this strain began were of an unknown sativa strain, possibly Thai, from Dan Christensen, who unfortunately passed away recently.

Interestingly enough, Madd Krush also shows blood-red pistils, although this coloring is much darker than the almost pink hues shown on Redd Cross. The colors seem to be a photogenic effect as this red is only expressed where the flowers are exposed to direct sunlight. Another trait shared with Redd Cross is the sturdiness of the plant; both the stalk and branches of this plant seem specifically designed to rival Arnie in bearing weights. Finishing fully in 14 weeks, this is a true sativa and does require some patience to let it reach its full maturity. This patience will be well rewarded, however, with the dank, dank buds that you'll get.

The dried buds of Madd Krush smell like Froot Loops with a taste to match, which is brilliant for anyone that misses that taste from childhood. The effect is a very cerebral one with a long duration. You'll enjoy a very active focus, which is the complete opposite of the effect of a bowl of Froot Loops, as you'll already know.

Genetics Gone Madd, USA

Sativa-Dominant

Genetics: Unknown sativa cross, possibly Thai

Potency: THC 19%

facebook.com/Genetics-GoneMad

Mako Haze

Kiwiseeds, the fantastic New Zealand breeders now based in the Netherlands, like to keep their cards close to their chest; in addition to the supreme genes of Northern Lights #5 and Haze, their Mako Haze strain comprises another set of genetics that they won't reveal. This secret ingredient is impressive, even if it is unknown, as Mako Haze gives a huge yield of super sticky buds that delight and tantalize all at the same time.

All fans of the queen of sativas, Haze, will love this plant, with its sativa growth habit and elongated branches. Able to grow happily in almost any situation, Mako Haze doesn't demand much from the grower except a slightly longer flowering time in order to reach its fullest potential. After the vegetative stage is over, give this plant 70 days and you'll find it straining under the weight of its own delicious-looking buds and desperate to be harvested. The dense clusters of bud will be sticky to the touch and dazzling to the eye. You'll be itching to trim, but remember to wear gloves when you start to harvest, or you might get a horribly strong contact high that sounds fun but isn't.

Kiwiseeds, Holland

Sativa-Dominant

Genetics: Unknown x (Northern Lights #5 x Haze)

Potency: THC 18%

kiwiseeds.com

Everyone loves the taste of Haze, and smokers of this strain will love the way the flavors play around their mouths. These nugs give a noticeably smooth smoke with a soaring feeling of "flying high" that lasts as long as you can handle.

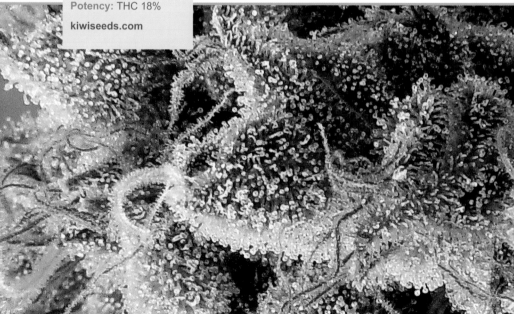

Margoot

Another of the fantastic Spanish seed companies that have been cropping up over the last ten years, Green Devil Genetics are known for coming out with very interesting crosses of well-known plants to create great original strains. Margoot comes from Maguma, which is a Mazar x Bubble Gum hybrid, that was bred with an Original Chocolate Thai plant. First produced several years ago, this strain has been preserved and stabilized and now enjoys a great reputation in Europe.

As an 85% sativa hybrid, Margoot forms very tall plants with lots of branches, so is best suited to a natural outdoor grow, although she can be tamed to grow indoors, too. This strain is acclimatized to the Mediterranean weather and will grow successfully in areas similar to this; if treated to lots of space, she can reward you with between 400 and 850 grams per plant when harvested in early November. Indoors, the flowering period lasts 10 or 11 weeks, so she takes a bit more patience than other strains, but gives a good harvest, too: about 50 grams per square foot indoors.

Green Devil Genetics, Spain

Sativa-Dominant

Genetics: Maguma x Chocolate Thai

Potency: THC 18-20%

greendevil.es

Growers often demand a lot of their plants if the flowering period is a long one, and this doesn't disappoint; the buds are very resinous and have a smell of incense that connoisseurs will love. The high is a balanced and positive head high that's both clear and exciting.

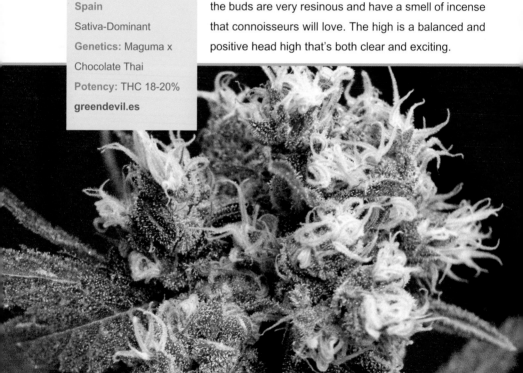

Maui

The excellently named Releaf Center is a Colorado medical dispensary dedicated to providing their patients with a wide variety of the best possible strains for their needs. They're constantly on the search for the best genetics, and they hit the jackpot with this landrace Hawaiian strain. Much like Molokai Frost, Maui is native to just one of the Hawaiian islands – and the fact that it's the most popular island with tourists who want to kick back and relax probably gives an indication of the effects of the strain, too. A pure sativa, this strain has grown wild on Maui for generations, and the island's

The Releaf Center, USA

Pure Sativa

Genetics: Landrace Hawaiian

Potency: THC 17%

thereleafcenter.com

diverse landscape has resulted in a unique and interesting plant – and one that's been popular since the 70s, thanks to the Cheech and Chong effect!

As a landrace sativa, this strain will always enjoy growing outdoors more than indoors, although it can be persuaded to do both. In its natural environment it will grow tall, up to 12 feet, but not too leggy, and indoors it will need some training if you don't want it to go crazy and declare the whole grow room as its own. Growing in containers under a 400-watt HPS or fluorescent lights can give great results indoors without compromising on the yield or flavors and it can be kept to under 4 feet if necessary. This plant can tolerate a certain amount of nutrients but they're unnecessary if you don't feel like expending the money or the effort. Maui can also be used in a ScrOG grow easily enough, but given that this strain is all about flavor, an organic soil grow can help to ensure the cleanest, most delicious smoke you can get. It has a longer flowering period of 9 to 10 weeks, but the final product is well worth the effort. The green and orange nugs look healthy and bright, and the average harvest is around 50 to 60 grams per plant.

Although this is not the most potent of strains, it's one that is layered in both taste and effects and should be enjoyed thoroughly. Think of it as a fine wine compared to a can of beer; it's more about the enjoyment of the complex flavor and experience rather than having shitloads of it and passing out or vomiting. The high begins with pressure in the forehead and behind the eyes, but then melts into a calm, clear high with enough push to get you through the day. Patients love Maui for its ability to ease the symptoms of carpal tunnel syndrome, glaucoma and depression, whereas everyone else loves it for its taste and wicked high.

Maxi Gom

Holland's Grass-O-Matic have created an incredible strain with Maxi Gom, a sativa-dominant hybrid of Critical + and AK-47 with a good dose of the Joint Doctor's ruderalis genetics in the mix, too. The ruderalis genes also make this killer strain an auto-flowering one, so she's great for beginner growers and those who don't have much time to devote to their crop.

To allow Maxi Gom to reach her full potential, the breeders recommend planting in pots larger than 10 to 12 liters and applying moderate amounts of fertilizer. The most fantastic growth, though, happens when Maxi Gom is placed in a hydro system indoors, where she can give a harvest of 50 grams per plant even in a small space. As with all auto-flowering varieties, the plant finishes quickly, with harvest occurring 75 days after germination whether grown indoors or outside. As the buds are long and tight, it is essential to keep an eye out for mold.

For a strain that is mostly sativa, Maxi Gom packs a heavy physical stone, making it a good medicinal strain, although your brain will definitely get a piece of the action, too. This is a great strain to to enjoy with friends when you want to be mentally stimulated but physically chilled, like when you've nothing to do but eat Cheetos and watch *Star Wars*.

PHOTOS BY DAVID STRANGE

Grass-O-Matic, Holland;
Grown by the Joint
Doctor, Canada
Sativa-Dominant
Genetics: Ruderalis x
Critical + x AK-47
Potency: THC 16-18%
grass-o-matic.com
lowryder.co.uk
jointdoctordirect.com

Mekong Haze

After nine years working within the Dutch cannabis industry, the guys at Delta 9 Labs started their company with the intent of creating an Earth-friendly business producing fantastic seeds. Their plants are all grown organically, and they boast a 100% germination rate when given the proper conditions. Their Mekong Haze is a pure landrace strain that grew wild in Southeast Asia, and as such, it is a particularly wild one to grow – but one that is well worth the effort.

The feral nature of this plant means that she is great for more experienced growers looking for a challenge. Mekong Haze enjoys hot and wet temperatures of about 95 degrees Fahrenheit, especially when the plants are small. She is recommended for breeding hybrid crosses and can serve as a great building block if you plan to create a brand new strain. Be aware that this strain takes up to 18 weeks to finish and will need a lot of room, but the end results will be well worth it. As they say, you can't keep a good woman down.

A motivating and clear smoke, Mekong Haze is one of those strains that dances around your head and makes you reach for the paint. The best move is to go along with this feeling and let your imagination go wild. Your Mekong Haze–driven creations may be frenzied and somewhat scatty, but hey – look at Jackson Pollock.

Delta 9 Labs, Holland

Pure Sativa

Genetics: Landrace Sativa from Southeast Asia

Potency: THC 18%

delta9labs.com

Moby Dick

In ten short years, Dinafem have risen to the top of the Spanish cannabis industry and don't show any signs of letting up. Moby Dick is their most well-known strain, a mix of fantastic Haze and White Widow genetics.

To get the very best out of your Moby Dick crop, it's essential to give the plants a lot of light; the breeders recommend 800 watts per square yard, and lots of feeding too. The pH should be lower than 6.5 at all times, or you risk iron deficiencies in the plants.

Dinafem Seeds, Spain

Sativa-Dominant

Genetics: Haze x White
Widow

Potency: THC 21%

dinafem.org

This will manifest in yellowing of the leaves, so be vigilant in checking your plants regularly and if the leaves start to yellow, adjust the pH accordingly. Outdoors, Moby Dick can grow to 10 feet if the plants are spaced 10 feet apart, and can harvest up to a massive 1500 grams in perfect conditions. Indoors, expect a flowering period of 60 to 70 days and a lighter yield than if grown outdoors.

Moby Dick is particularly psychoactive (I bet that phrase doesn't appear in Melville's book!) and is a definite quick-hitter. You'll be "up" almost instantly, and after a period of both mental and physical energy you'll slide into a very chill, lengthy and enjoyable comedown.

NYC Diesel

I've never quite understood why Holland's Soma Seeds don't sell a T-shirt that apes the famous New York one, but instead reads "I Heart NYC Diesel" with a cheeky shot of bud behind the heart; tourists might get a more interesting keepsake and every patriotic pothead could praise their favorite strain! With the combined genetics of a Mexican sativa and an Afghani indica, NYC Diesel is Soma's most famous strain, and one that has its roots in some seeds bought by a dreadlocked friend in the Big Apple itself.

This strain grows to about 4 feet in height and doesn't usually cause any trouble for even novice growers; mild-mannered and easy to please, she has a good resistance to pests and doesn't demand heavy nutrient applications. After a manageable 11-week flowering period you can expect a harvest of at least 25 grams per plant indoors, which is a great yield for such minimal effort. If you'd like to get a mother plant (and you will), clones are ridiculously easy to get – and almost impossible to kill.

Despite the name, NYC Diesel's aromas are more ripe grapefruit than slick oil. This strain has a 40% indica profile so the high is balanced between head and body. Soma's recommendation is to enjoy NYC Diesel with a good meal – and if you're in NYC, there's no shortage of those. Just don't break down and get one of those hot dogs.

Soma Seeds, Holland

Sativa-Dominant

Genetics: Mexican Sativa x Afghani

Potency: THC 20%

somaseeds.nl

Oldtimes

Underground Originals have a special place in my heart, not just because their website says that they sell art, but because their nickname, Ugorg, sounds to me like the cumbersome, simple and ineffective Transformer that never was. In reality, these guys provide strains passed down to them through generations and use landrace genetics that have been collected for over 40 years by Oldtimer1, the daddy of this company. If that's not an assurance of quality, I don't know what is.

Oldtimes is a seriously old-school variety bred from the enigmatic ESB and ES strains. Its parent plants can have tendencies towards hermaphroditism when put under stress, so try to keep Oldtimes as chilled out as possible and keep a sharp eye out for any male flowering after transplanting. Growth will be fairly rapid and the buds will have hardly any leaves. Flowering sits at around 8 to 9 weeks.

Your Oldtimes buds won't be as pungent as ESB, but they'll certainly give off a distinctive whiff as soon as you get near them. The high is almost all in the head, with a little leakage down to the body just so it doesn't feel left out. After it's settled down a little, your overactive mind will start reminiscing about the old days when pot was pot and a dollar could buy you a car – but don't worry about this, it's fairly normal.

Underground Originals, UK

Sativa-Dominant

Genetics: ESB x ES

Potency: THC 18%

ugorg.com

Onyx

Being a person of diminutive height, I feel like Short Stuff Seeds are the company for me. A lot of taller people have the same feeling though, which I'm sure has a lot more to do with the breeding collective's high-grade strains like Himalaya Blue Diesel than any feeling of solidarity with us shorties. In the few years that they've been working together, the enthusiasts at Short Stuff have been primarily working with ruderalis genetics to create a range of auto-flowering plants, and with Onyx, they've created an auto-flowering sativa-dominant hybrid that brings together some of the best strains of recent times. AK-47 and White Russian, both from Serious Seeds, and Soma Seeds' NYC Diesel have been brought together by breeder Stitch and then crossed with a secret ruderalis-influenced plant to ensure taste, potency and vigor, all in an auto-flowering plant. I can see why the tall people like them.

The trend with most auto-flowering plants is for them to be indica-dominant, and though Onyx may look like it is small enough to be an indica, it is in fact sativa-dominant. Growing only to around 3 feet in height, this taming of the normal sativa growth pattern is great news for indoor growers who want the sativa high from a more compact grow. However, it's important to keep the lights close to the seedlings when they're in the vegetative stage so as not to encourage stretch. The plants grow fat with branching but don't become difficult to maintain, and as their maturation is genetically determined, you can be harvesting between 25 and 50 grams of sick bud per plant within 10 weeks from seed.

Short Stuff Seeds,
breeder Stitch, Spain
Auto-Flowering Sativa-
Dominant
Genetics: AK-47 x White
Russian x NYC Diesel x
Unknown Strain
Potency: THC 18%
shortstuffseeds.com

When harvest time rolls around you'll notice a distinctly Skunk-esque smell about your grow room, so be sure to take extra measures to contain that telltale aroma: carbon filters and ventilation to an inconspicuous area usually do the trick. Onyx fares particularly well in a soil grow that's been treated with good quality additives, but remember if you are using nutrients that you should flush for at least a week before harvest to get the best taste possible.

Though there is some indica influence in this plant, the smoke is all sativa. The light smoke has a fruity taste that's also citrusy in places and gets more and more complex as you toke. The high is a medium-strong 'up,' one that's very clear; a good choice for a daytime smoke if you have to actually do things rather than just bouncing around like Tigger on ADHD meds.

Orient Express

Spain's ACE Seeds is a collective of breeders and cannabis lovers who focus on preserving heirloom and landrace strains and breeding the best new varieties from their quality breeding stock. Orient Express is currently one of their most popular strains, and rightly so; Vietnam Black is a pure sativa strain from Southeast Asia, while China Yunnan is a mostly-indica hybrid hailing from the home of Confucius and the Tao. By breeding these two stellar strains together, ACE Seeds have shortened the flowering time of Vietnam Black but kept the high production and the beautiful aromatics, and have thus created the best of both worlds in one plant – and isn't that what makes a killer breeder?

This strain is best suited to subtropical climates if it's being grown outdoors, but if you are not in a subtropical area, coastal climates can also harbor good crops of Orient Express – take advantage of the warm fall growing conditions when you can! However, this strain is fairly resistant to cold, but shouldn't be exposed unnecessarily. This is a variety that's recommended for sativa lovers with smaller gardens, who may not have success growing larger South Asian plants in their limited space. The landrace Chinese Yunnan influence helps this plant stay small with a compact structure and a good amount of branching without impacting too much on the rate of production.

ACE Seeds, Spain

Sativa-Dominant

Genetics: Vietnam Black x China Yunnan

Potency: THC 14-16%

aceseeds.org

Due to the potent aroma and delicious taste of the finished bud, it might be a good idea to grow Orient Express entirely organically, as chemical feeding and excessive additives can dull the flavors of more tasty bud, and you want your final harvest to be the best it can possibly be. If growing this plant outdoors, you should be looking to harvest at around the start of October. The flowering period lasts 9 weeks, which of course is longer than most indicas but is on the faster end of the sativa flowering spectrum.

You'll be basking in the aroma of your maturing buds from halfway through the flowering stage, but once you've harvested and cured your finished nugs you'll be astounded at the smell, which is exactly like a damp rainforest full of flowers. Earthy and floral, the smoke is light and brings on a very clear, very smooth sativa high without any paranoia. This feels like the stuff you smoked on your trip around the world, when you were in Bangkok with that guy who looked like Jack Black, just before you bought that Thai rum and everything went downhill.

OZone

TreeTown Seeds are a brilliant U.S.-based company currently providing high-quality seeds to the medical marijuana community in San Francisco. They're also producing some great strains and have been doing so for the last few years, so it's high time that they get some recognition for their hard work and the great success they've been having with their varieties. Created back in 2009 but not introduced until 2011, OZone was born of a Sensi Seeds Northern Lights #1 plant that got romantic with an AK-47

TreeTown Seeds, USA

Sativa-Dominant

Genetics: (Northern Lights x AK-47) x AK-47

Potency: THC 14.54-21.09%

treetownseeds.com

from Serious Seeds. This plant had a very strong hazelnut flavor, and was backcrossed into itself when the right mother plant was found. Developed as a "big bud" plant, OZone hit all the targets that the breeders had aimed for: size, THC content and a flowering time of 60 days or less. It couldn't have been more perfect.

There are two phenotypes currently expressed from OZone, one known as the Cherry pheno and the other known as the Monster pheno. The Cherry pheno retains the nutty flavor of its mother but has a taste that wanders into berry country, and so was nicknamed Cherry by the breeders. The Monster pheno, on the other hand, concerns itself less with taste but more with some insane growth, resulting in a huge size and a great bud-to-leaf ratio. The breeder's recommendation for both phenotypes is to let them grow naturally, as they've been bred to have a fantastic structure enabling them to hold their own weight even towards the end of flowering. Bugs are also a non-issue, thanks to the resistance of the Northern Lights genetics, and the flowering time is just under 60 days, so mold shouldn't get to take hold either. One important breeder's tip is to invest in a 30x microscope, as the trichomes will go milky and be finished before the stigmas at the ends of the pistils die, so it is best to harvest around 56 days, when 80% of the stigmas are still cloudy. Yield should be around 550 grams per square yard of grow space.

The high of both phenotypes is very social and uplifting, although the uninitiated smoker might find themselves dropping to the floor and being a little too overwhelmed to get up! Remember when toking that the AK-47 parent strain is named for its ability to get you totally shot with only a few tries, so take it easy when you first pack a bowl. This is a great strain for socializing and it keeps you on the go forever.

Pablo's Cheese

British company Cannaseur Seeds have certainly raised the bar with this strain. The Colombian Goldbud genetics that form the basis for this strain were collected by the breeders back in 2002 on their travels in the north of Colombia, at great risk to the breeders. Goldbud is an extreme equatorial sativa, never hybridized, which takes upwards of 18 weeks from the start of the flowering period to fully mature. The other parent, The Cheese, was cut from an original UK clone mother and has been grown by the Cannaseur breeders for many years. The resulting Pablo's Cheese was such a success that in 2009, the project to create a population of F2s was undertaken. These buds are 75% sativa in growing style and 80% sativa in smoke.

Generations of rigorous selection have made Pablo's Cheese very resistant to mold so she can be taken through wet periods in an outdoor grow without any problems, and is great indoors as well. Outdoors, this strain will make the most of the extra room and fresh air, blooming into a gorgeous plant that will be the envy of any other backyard growers. Though the plants will be smaller and more tame indoors, they will still display phenomenal growth. The taller phenotypes of this strain can have larger intermodal spacing than all the others, so be sure to keep your lights close to these plants in the seedling and vegetative stages to avoid any unnecessary stretch that would make them even leggier. If you do find yourself with a plant that is a little large for your indoor grow space, these ladies can respond well to LST. The breeders strongly recommend that this strain should not be subjected to any chemicals, so an organic soil grow is best. It's important to be aware that, as a Cheese strain, this one will stink up your whole house near to harvest time. Invest in some good filters and ensure good ventilation if you don't want the cops from the next county knocking on your door.

Cannaseur Seeds, UK;
Breeder Pistils and Co.
Sativa-Dominant
Genetics: Colombian
Goldbud x The Cheese
Potency: THC 20%
breedbay.co.uk
cannaseur.co.uk

Each different expression in the F2 generation of Pablo's Cheese differs slightly, but all offer an energetic, positive, dreamy high that is definitely felt above the shoulders. The fine, Skunky, cheesy taste is delicious and the high hits hard from the first intake. Be aware that the effects are very deep and long lasting, so plan ahead: settle in with a new videogame and a minifridge full of treats and fruit – and remember to keep it within arm's length! This is a connoisseur's strain through and through, and even experienced growers will love to cultivate Pablo.

Psicodelicia

Spain's Sweet Seeds pride themselves on the quality of their products and the way they make growing accessible to people of any budget; they sell seeds in packs of 3 and 5 as well as 10, so if you've only got a few bucks to spare then you're not out of the game! They love to breed great-tasting strains, and Psicodelicia (*see-ko-del-ee-see-ah*), which means psychedelic in Spanish, is not only tasty, but trippy to boot. Having got hold of a cutting of a mysterious crossbred plant from the U.S., the breeders at Sweet Seeds decided to mate this with a landrace sativa from the heart of Nepal that has an amazing aroma of ground coffee. The landrace genetics made the already great U.S. cutting go nice and wild, with hugely increased vigor and tolerance with a larger harvest at the end of it all.

Grown from clone, Psicodelicia roots fully in about a week thanks to the landrace genetics. From seed the strain loses none of this vitality and can reach 10 inches within just a few days if it's given plenty of light. However, remember to keep the lights close to the seedlings at all times, or they will stretch rather than grow properly formed, and that will result in a leggy plant that's difficult to tend to. As a heavy sativa-dominant this will grow tall, but after a fairly short vegetative stage it should fill out well in the flowering stage and use all the space you've given it. It adapts well to different environments and resists both pests and diseases as well as stress. You also shouldn't need to use fertilizer as long as the soil is of good quality.

Sweet Seeds, Spain

Sativa-Dominant

Genetics: Nepali Landrace x Unknown Hybrid

Potency: THC 15-20%

sweetseeds.es

During the last 2 weeks of flowering the buds will suddenly become wrapped In resin that will make it very difficult to wait until they're properly mature! If you're growing this strain in a grow room, your plants will be finished in about 9 weeks and if you've treated them well, they will give you a harvest of around 500 grams per square yard of grow room. The landrace genetics make the plants go crazy outdoors, so in this instance you should be able to harvest 700 grams per plant at the end of September. You'll be a popular cat all the way through the fall with a stash like that.

As the name might suggest, Psicodelicia is a very sativa-like high. It's almost entirely cerebral with a little body tingle, but you won't even notice what your legs are doing because your head will be on another planet, unable to recognize its surroundings and making futile attempts to form words that the creatures around it can understand.

Quasar

Spain's Buddha Seeds are highly thought of in the Spanish cannabis community and rightly so; their mixes of indica and sativa genetics never disappoint, and tend to exhibit the best of both species. Quasar is one of these hybrids, and counts a pure indica plant and a backcrossed sativa as its parents. The result is a plant that can be grown indoors or outdoors with astonishing results.

With vigorous growth and a super-strong structure, Quasar is ready to yield some huge buds from the moment it begins germination. These buds, when they emerge, are both dense and compact, putting the branches under a challenging amount of weight. However, this plant can certainly handle itself, and all a grower needs to do is make sure it is fed enough and check regularly for mold within the ever-increasing buds. An easy one to grow, Quasar also gives a very satisfying yield. It may not be the greatest producer, but the quality of the harvested bud certainly makes up for that.

The confidence given by a Quasar smoke matches the attitude with which it grows, and the euphoria you feel won't be tempered by the usual paranoia, leaving you to bask in the glow of the exhilarating rush that's searing a path through your mind and body. This is the kind of high that makes you want to go for a bike ride, just to feel the wind in your face – but probably stay away from busy roads or highways.

Buddha Seeds, Spain

Sativa-Dominant

Genetics: Pure Indica x Sativa BX

Potency: THC 18%

buddhaseedbank.com

hemptrading.com

Sage 'N Sour

Based in the Netherlands, T.H. Seeds take the breeding game pretty seriously. Their favorite strain, S.A.G.E.– or Sativa Afghani Genetic Equilibrium, to give it its full name – is so loved in the TH Seeds labs that they would have never dreamed of pairing it with a substandard plant. In fact, the only suitor to have passed their extensive questioning was infamous Sour Diesel, which has a genetic history so rich that we would have to release its long form birth certificate to even come close to mentioning it all. From this beautiful union came Sage 'N Sour, and with a shorter flowering time than S.A.G.E. and a bigger yield than Sour Diesel, it's got the best of both worlds.

This is a sativa-dominant variety, and doesn't stay small for long. It isn't unusual for these plants to grow to 5 feet, so they are well-suited for outdoor growth or for deep water culture setups indoors. After 9 weeks flowering, you should be looking at a yield of around 350 grams per square yard of grow room, and your buds will look like little Christmas presents by harvest time: red, green and shimmering all over.

T.H. Seeds, Holland

Sativa-Dominant

Genetics: S.A.G.E. x Sour Diesel

Potency: THC 18%

thseeds.com

Sage 'N Sour's taste also comprises the best of both parents, though it has more citrus and less fuel flavors than you might expect. The high is mostly in the head, and almost pulls you out of your seat with the strength of its uplifting power.

Santa Maria F8

No Mercy Supply are a Netherlands-based seed company that are very serious about producing quality strains, as their F8 cut of Santa Maria shows. This strain originates in the Brazilian Amazon, and is used spiritually by the people in that area. No Mercy crossed a Santa Maria plant with a Mexican Haze and a Silver Pearl, then back-crossed this for four generations. A male from that generation was then bred with a pure Santa Maria mother, which was then inbred 8 times by backcrossing a male with the mother plant.

Originally an outdoor plant, Santa Maria is happiest outside under natural light. However, even outdoors you should cut her back, otherwise she'll keep growing and growing and will eventually succumb to the weight of her flowers, even with additional staking. Cutting vertically will encourage outward growth and result in a bushier plant that can hold itself better. Expect a flowering time of about 60 days.

This generation of Santa Maria is said to have very strong erotic effects, and as such, should be used with caution. I'm not sure whether these effects take the form of super potent pheromones emanating from the smoker, or manifest themselves as an incredibly sexy atmosphere in the room, but either way, be careful who you attract and remember to play safe.

No Mercy Supply,
Holland

Sativa-Dominant

Genetics: Pure Santa Maria

nomercy.nl

antiontehkhd.com

Shining Silver Haze

With over two decades of experience in the growing industry, the guys at Royal Queen Seeds in the Netherlands have more than enough knowledge to produce some fantastic strains for all levels of cultivator. Their products have won much respect over the years and Shining Silver Haze is a variety that certainly demands some attention. Though the exact genetic composition is a closely guarded secret, we do know that this strain is a rare, sativa-dominant member of the Haze family that began life in the U.S. in the marijuana heyday of the 70s. We also know that it is a blend of Colombian, Mexican, Thai and Jamaican plants that bring power in both growth and smoke as well as a whole ruck of juicy, potent buds.

If you're an indoor grower with a limited amount of space, Shining Silver Haze might be a perfect choice for a productive grow. With a maximum height of just under 3 feet, it fits into most smaller grow rooms and can yield up to 450 grams per square yard of grow space. The flowering time has also been reduced; whereas pure Haze varieties sometimes take as long as 14 weeks to finish, Shining Silver Haze will be ready in just 9. The plants are tolerant to nutrients but can burn if you feed them excessively, so be sure to keep a close eye on the color and shape of your leaves – yellowing or other discoloration can be a sign that you're giving them just too much.

Royal Queen Seeds,
Holland
Sativa-Dominant
Genetics: Colombian x
Mexican x Thai x
Jamaican
Potency: THC 20%
royalqueenseeds.com

Though this strain was designed primarily as an indoor plant, she won't exactly be annoyed if you plant her outdoors; just make sure that you give her lots of water if you're growing in a warmer climate and disguise your plants as much as possible; even if you're a legal grower there are predators other than the law waiting to pop your crop! These plants can also adapt well to a deep water culture set up. If you choose to go down this route, or any hydro set up, you should be rigorous in checking your grow every day and monitoring all variables; it's easy for one thing to go wrong and ruin your grow before you know what's happening.

Every toker loves a Haze high, and this one has the added bonus of bringing on a fierce body stone as well as the usual mind melt. Shining Silver Haze almost has the effect of pulling you in two different directions; it makes your body heavier and your mind lighter, which might make you feel like you're on something of an emotional rack, but hey, it's an enjoyable ride!

Simbay Moon

Ganjah Seeds are a great young company operating out of San Sebastian in Spain, who spend their time drinking sangria and growing killer weed. Simbay Moon is one of their original strains, and was bred from a Mexican sativa plant and a beautiful Afghani indica. This union resulted in a sativa-dominant with great genes and bags of personality.

The Mexican sativa influence in Simbay Moon gives a very tall plant with quite a bit of stretch, but the calming influence of the Afghani genetics makes this hybrid easier to handle than you might expect. There's a lot of very vigorous growth here but the stalk is thick and sturdy with a fantastic root structure, so Simbay Moon can certainly hold its own. This might not be true later on in flowering, however, with the large buds weighing down the branches, making it necessary to stake or otherwise support your plant until it's ready for harvest time. Outdoors this guy can grow up to ten feet, though indoors, a little training can keep it at least a few feet shorter.

Once harvest time does roll around, in mid-October, you'll be intoxicated by the exotic, fruity aromas of the cured bud before you even get a chance to smoke them up. That first toke, however, will hit you like a 6-foot wave and plant you face first into a cerebral, active high that carries a good amount of body stone once the energy has worn off.

Ganjah Seeds, Spain

Sativa-Dominant

Genetics: Mexican Sativa x Afghani

Potency: THC 16%

ganjahseeds.net

Skunk #1

Peak Seeds are based in the cannabis hotspot of Canada's British Columbia, and are as passionate about preserving good genetics as they are about customer service. It makes sense, then, that they would carry such a high-quality version of what has been referred to as the most popular strain in the world – pure Skunk. Skunk #1 comes from a mix of Colombian and Mexican genetics with some Afghani genes, and as anyone will tell you, it is a treat to smoke.

With some indica influence, Skunk #1 exhibits very vigorous growth, especially after the vegetative stage, and enjoys a flowering period of 8 to 9 weeks. If left untopped, these plants tend to grow a huge central cola and prefer a slightly more damp soil mix than some other strains. You can expect the plants to grow to about 4 feet indoors although they can grow much larger outside.

When they're ready for harvest your crop will have that inimitable stench, the Skunk smell that everyone knows and loves — so you will have to invest in some charcoal air filters to get rid of the smell or all your neighbors will know what you're up to! Once dried, the bud will give a lemony, dense smoke with a very "up" high that's full of energy and makes you feel amazing. Those neighbors will probably be coming over for a toke, too!

Peak Seeds, Canada

Sativa-Dominant

Genetics: Afghani x Colombian x Mexican

Potency: THC 17%

peakseedsbc.com

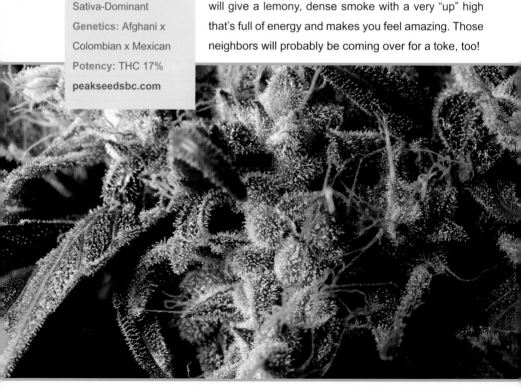

Skunkenstein

Project Skunkenstein is a private breeder in Australia, working hard to produce incredible original strains with interesting genetics. I'm a sucker for a well-named chunk of good bud, so I loved this strain before I knew anything else about it, but this is no gimmick; Skunkenstein was born of some phenomenal landrace genetics originally from Nepal.

A sativa-dominant hybrid, Skunkenstein shares its growth patterns with Frankenstein's monster; once you get it started, it really takes on a life of its own. The sativa genes mean that it will grow as large as the room allows, but rather than being horrified by what you've created, you'll be more than impressed. If you can handle the pressure, Skunkenstein loves to be cloned and without much effort you can have a whole army of uniform, baby Skunkensteins growing like monsters, without even having to build your monster a mate.

This strain is as wild in your head as it is in your garden: highly cerebral and full of a ridiculous amount of energy. The vigor of the plants seems to be transferred from the bud to you! Just be careful that you don't end up with a talking Skunkenstein plant that's lamenting its own existence and sending you on a mission up to the Arctic (read the book).

Project Skunkenstein, Australia

Sativa-Dominant

Genetics: Nepali Landrace

Potency: THC 18%

thcfarmer.com

Sonoma Sunrise

BillBerry Farms, based in the U.S., is a company passionate about providing tissue cultures rather than seeds. Working with tissue culture is thought to be even smoother than working with clones, and when you're dealing with a strain like Sonoma Sunrise, quality and ease are important! An original BillBerry strain, this is a cross between a NY Sour Diesel and Mendocino Purp hybrid and a mix of OG Kush and Pineapple Thai plants.

Though this strain can grow well in the heat of its native area, it doesn't enjoy being too hot indoors and you should take measures to keep your grow room cool. If you are working with limited space, the breeder recommends switching to 12 on/12 off as soon as the plant reaches your desired height. Be sure to keep the nitrates up all the way through the grow. As this plant nears its perfect harvest time the buds will exhibit both purple and orange shades, and should be fully finished around 8 weeks after forced flowering. Expect to get 180 grams per plant or 350 grams outdoors.

Sonoma Sunrise buds have an aroma of ripened pineapple from the Pineapple Thai grandparent and the high affects both head and body equally, as any good hybrid should. The high is luxuriously long lasting and relaxes the whole body, making it a excellent strain for medical marijuana users with physical pain or discomfort.

PHOTOS BY JIN ALBRECHT AND BBF

BillBerry Farms, USA

Sativa-Dominant

Genetics: (NY Sour Diesel x Mendocino Purp) x (OG Kush x Pineapple Thai)

billberryfarmstissue-culture.com

Sour Amnesia

Using mainly European and North American genetics to create some awesome new strains, Holland's HortiLab have become known for coming up with plants that deliver potency, flavor and yield all at the same time. Known especially for their Sour strains, they are constantly working to introduce new varieties to the market, but Sour Amnesia is one of their existing strains that has already gained much attention. East Coast Sour Diesel was bred in order to be the true representation of the infamous Sour Diesel strain, offered in seed form, and it took almost three years to perfect. As an inbred line of Sour Diesel, ECSD can count ChemDawg, Northern Lights and several versions of Skunk in its family. Conversely, Amnesia, from the original Holland cut, is of the Super Silver Haze family with Haze, Skunk, and Northern Lights influences.

Sour Amnesia plants are known to be especially good for commercial production – although I only advocate this in countries where cultivation is legal, of course. Though the flowering time sits at around 11 weeks, the sheer weight of the yield is enough for commercial growers to choose this strain – even indoor growers can expect to harvest at least 60 grams of bud per square yard of grow space. The yield increases if the plants are grown outdoors, so long as thieves or cops don't get their grubby hands on your crop: remember that vigilance is key! Growers with a lot of experience with different strains also enjoy Sour Amnesia crops, as they produce large colas made up of very dense buds that have a fantastic depth of aroma. Adaptable to most kinds of growing techniques, these plants enjoy a lot of feeding, but be sure to ease up if the leaves start to droop, as this can be a sign that you've gone a little overboard.

HortiLab Seed Company, Holland

Sativa-Dominant

Genetics: East Coast Sour Diesel x Amnesia

Potency: THC 18%

hortilab.nl

These might just be the dankest of dank buds that you've ever had a whiff of; the Amnesia stink has distinct undertones of oil that forms one of those "you have to smell it for yourself" aromas. They'll also be coated so heavily from top to tail in a thick layer of resinous crystals that if you leave the buds too long a rapper might pick them up and wear them as jewelry. I know this won't happen though; as soon as your buds are cured you'll be grinding those beauties and rolling a fat one without even a thought for their attractiveness, and I can't blame you. Their smoke is a very crisp one with a very well-defined tangy flavor, and before long the creeper of the head high will make itself felt and you'll find out why they call this family Amnesia. Remember that if you wake up with no memory, you probably had a good time.

South African Landrace

I was absolutely stoked when I found out that the fantastic Autofem Seeds of Spain had got hold of some South African Landrace genetics and were using them as breeding stock. Autofem's breeder has traveled the world sourcing great genetics and his excellent strains exemplify his passion for quality breeding stock like this Landrace South African beauty.

This plant has been used in several of their commercial hybrids, and in development with auto-flowering strains to produce some much-needed auto-flowering sativas. These landrace plants grow wild and unruly in their natural habitat and they are huge – with some reaching 14 or 15 feet in height! However, as they're constantly being subjected to the natural airflow of the wind, their stalks and branches are incredibly strong. Autofem have done well in stabilizing this landrace strain through to F11 versions that express only one phenotype and have been fully tamed.

If you ever buddy up with the lovely Autofem guys and you're lucky enough to get

Autofem Seeds, Spain

Pure Sativa

Genetics: Landrace South African

autofem.com

some South African Landrace buds from them, be ready for a trip that sends you sideways, backwards and inside out like no other pot you've smoked before. Just be sure to practice good manners, African-style, and thank them for their Ubuntu.

Cannabis Sativa The Essential Guide to the World's Finest Marijuana Strains

Strawberry Crème

America's Riot Seeds have done it again with this super rare sativa-dominant with some fantastic grow traits and a taste that will blow your mind. Though Strawberry Crème began life as the Swiss strain Erdbeer (which means strawberry, funnily enough), this strain has been backcrossed and stabilized and is now available in seed form from Riot Seeds. Thanks to its amazing flavor and buds that are coated with resin, this strain is getting more and more popular every day and is even over-taking other classic Strawberry strains in the fame stakes. Watch out for a big fat joint of it on the front of *Time* magazine before too long, being smoked by Lady Gaga or Justin Bieber or whatever insipid eunuch they wheel out as the next media mon-ster. Not that I'm bitter.

Although Strawberry Crème is almost pure sativa, the breeders at Riot Seeds have managed to bring the flowering time down to 10 weeks, which is a good while shorter than other sativa-heavy strains on the market. It is happiest in an organic soil grow in which its natural flavors are allowed to flour-ish, and it's a heavy yielder so don't be afraid to help it along with some organic nutrients and a hell of a lot of light. The plants may need a little supporting nearer har-vest so it can be a good idea to stake them early on, while it's still easy to get to the stalks. By the end of the flowering period the nugs will be fairly pale but glittering with white crystals and the size of the harvest will leave you utterly shocked: it's a monster yielder.

Riot Seeds, USA

Sativa-Dominant

Genetics: Clone only

Swiss Strawberry BX

Potency: THC 19%

riotseeds.nl

You know when you're at those fancy parties dying for a beer and a burger, but the caterers keep handing you mini toasts loaded with some indistinguishable fish-based spread and glasses of crap champagne with a strawberry on the side? Well, next time, just politely suggest to the host that they should bring round a stack of joints packed with Strawberry Crème instead – it tastes just the same and if they grow their own, it'll save them a hell of a lot of cash. They'll also save money on the food, as no one will want foie gras or caviar; they'll just want a bag of chips, a couple of cans of cheap, crap beer and another joint. It will also be a much more fun party, as everyone will be high as white clouds and discussing the merits of *Star Wars* and doing wookie impressions. As if that's not good enough, this strain is also helpful in treating prob-lems like depression and nausea – which incidentally are both issues you can get from listening to the aforementioned artists at crap parties.

Superbomb

America's Alphakronik Genes are a new-school company known for their great varieties and reliable genetics. Superbomb is a backcross version of the celebrated Spacequeen, and in creating this strain, AKG wanted to maintain the best traits of the fabulous parent plant. They have definitely succeeded with Superbomb.

Having picked Spacequeen's flavor and the phenotypes that grew trichome-laden buds as their favorite traits, the breeders at AKG decided to focus on expressing these characteristics in their hybrid and took two years doing so. The result is a plant that happily grows to 5 feet but doesn't exhibit much stretch, and flowers in 65 days indoors. If growing outdoors, the harvest date for this is around the end of September, and you'll find the finished buds very easy to manicure with few leaves around the bud sites.

The Superbomb smoke is so sweet it's like a chunk of vanilla sugar dipped in honey and delivered by a Powerpuff Girl singing *On The Good Ship Lollipop*. The effects sit somewhere between sativa and indica types, with a mild body stone and a bit of a brain buzz, too. For this reason this strain can be helpful for a range of mental and physical conditions, including insomnia, IBS and Crohn's disease. It's also great as an all-round high for anyone with a sweet tooth and a penchant for a chillaxing evening.

Alphakronik Genes, USA

Sativa-Dominant

Genetics: Spacequeen F1 x Spacequeen F2

Potency: THC 12-15%

cannabis-seeds-bank.co.uk

rollitup.org

Super Haze

Ch9 Female Seeds are a great and well renowned company in Europe who've been putting out great strains for longer than I've been smoking. For this strain, the company's own Jack33 was bred with Mr. Nice's Super Silver Haze, a strain that in itself comprises the Hall of Fame of cannabis genetics. Super Haze enjoys a heritage that's a blend of Haze, Skunk, Northern Lights #5 and Jack Herer, with some G-13, Kali Mist and G Bolt genetics coming from the Jack33 parent. You can see why they call it Super.

Introduced back in 2007, Super Haze is a 70-30 sativa-indica hybrid that is suitable for both indoor and outdoor grows in both hot and cold climates. Outdoors, the plants can grow up to 9 feet, and have a flowering time of 8-9 weeks. The ease of growing this plant makes it a good choice for cultivators of all skill levels, and the breeder recommends that growers do not over-fertilize the plant. The breeder also recommends feeding with tepid water for the best results, and spreading the branches when it's harvest time, to allow for an easy chop. This strain is great for closets and gardens, but is a limited series, so get it while you can!

Ch9 Female Seeds,
Europe
Sativa-Dominant
Genetics: Super Silver
Haze x Ch9 Jack33
Potency: THC 17-20%
ch9femaleseeds.com

The Super Haze taste is a very floral and citrusy one, leading into a high that leaves you almost literally flying, with the psychedelic and uplifting feelings baffling your senses in a most welcome way.

Thai

Original Seeds is a fantastic breeders' collective located in a remote part of Russia whose dedication to finding and preserving landrace plants is second to none. As such, this Thai plant is a landrace sativa originally selected from Sahon Nakhon, in the northeast of Thailand near the border with Laos. This plant belongs to the traditional Thai family of cannabis and exhibits a huge number of trichomes and dense inflorescences as well as a high flower-to-leaf ratio. Original Seeds never mixes this Thai strain with plants from any other locality, even other Thais, in order to retain the pure, unadulterated and high-quality sativa genetics that everyone so loves.

This Thai strain is an especially vigorous one when allowed to develop in outdoor cultivation. It can, however, be grown smaller and indoors, although this of course has some impact on the size of the harvest. It fairs particularly well if given 13 hours of light while still a seedling. This can be shortened to 11 hours after a couple of weeks. These conditions mirror the natural, and therefore ideal, conditions of its Thai homeland and will provide you with a fantastic harvest. Though the first leaves on these plants will be irregular and twisted, the later leaves are more uniform.

Original Seeds, Russia

Pure Sativa

Genetics: Landrace Thai

originalseeds.org

As a mountainous Thai plant, this variety will exhibit purplish stems when they start to grow and will then branch out well, negating the need for cropping. Colas will form on all of the side branches in gorgeous abundance, so you might need to stake the plant towards the later stages of flowering to help it carry that huge crop. Another trait that sets this pure strain apart from many Thai hybrids is the absence of hermaphrodites; even stressing the plant with transplanting and the like will not cause hermies – which is great news for any grower. This Thai can be cut after 50 days of flowering, but in order to bring out the real psychoactive qualities, the breeder recommends leaving it for 80 days of flowering so it can be well ripened and at its best for you to smoke.

This variety contains almost no CBD and a high percentage of THC, so the effect is very different from conventional hybrids; there is no knockout, no ceiling and no paranoia at all. The smoke tastes unusually sweet for a Thai, and, especially if you allow for a longer flowering period, you will find yourself in an extremely positive, psychedelic world that may be far from reality in places but will definitely be a place you'll want to stay. If you take only small doses the mental action will pass soon enough, and you can start all over again as soon as you wish – with even better effects the second time around. There is no limit to how good this high can get!

Thai Lights

Dr. Atomic, a breeder based in Canada, has traveled extensively, collecting the best genetics from all over the world to form the basis for his original strains. By crossing a Haze plant from Nakan Pranom in northeast Thailand with his own Atomic Northern Lights strain – an indica-dominant plant with a prolonged, intense high – he has created the potent and energizing Thai Lights.

The second generation of this strain is shorter, grows more vigorously and gives greater yields than its predecessor, making it both easier and more fun to grow. With more influence from its Atomic Northern Lights parent, the plant grows very bushy for a sativa-dominant and as such, grows well in operations with restricted space. Maintaining the fantastic Thai Haze profile, this strain flowers indoors in about 10 weeks, and gives an eventual harvest of 60 grams per plant if treated with plenty of light.

Not for the rookie smoker, Thai Lights is noticeably strong, though its sweet taste and light smoke might fool you into thinking the opposite. Thankfully it's a cerebral high that gives you tons of energy rather than putting you out for the evening, so you don't have to worry about being a totally antisocial potato if you go a bit overboard. Although you should probably be aware that bouncing off the walls around sober people can be a bit annoying, too.

Dr. Atomic Seedbank,
Canada
Sativa-Dominant
Genetics: Thai Haze x
Atomic Northern Lights
Potency: THC 20%
dratomicseedbank.com
vancouverseedbank.ca

The Bulldog Haze

The Bulldog coffeeshop was one of the first to open in Amsterdam, having first started life as an underground smokers' den that had 'counterculture' written right through its bones. Thirty-four years after The Bulldog opened, the guys decided to team up with some of the world's best breeders and produce a range of their own seeds - and so The Bulldog Seeds was born. With so much competition the guys had a big challenge ahead of them, and they rose to it with ease; their original strains such as this, The Bulldog Haze, prove that they're still ahead of the game. The breeders began with some fantastic genetics from that other Amsterdam mega-company, Green House, and with two fantastic sativa-hybrids under their arms they cultivated a new classic. Green House's Lemon Skunk came from the most popular strain ever, Skunk #1, while their Super Silver Haze is a mix of Skunk, Haze and NL#5 genetics that never disappoints. Blending these two super-plants together formed a sativa-dominant strain that's a high yielder and a great smoke.

The Bulldog Seeds,
Holland

Sativa-Dominant

Genetics: Lemon Skunk x
Super Silver Haze

Potency: THC 19%

bulldogseeds.nl

As a more balanced hybrid, The Bulldog Haze doesn't exhibit the extreme growth patterns that more sativa-heavy blends sometimes can. For that reason, this plant is suitable for both indoor and outdoor grows, and can even be a good choice for those short on grow space and needing to be stealthy. It's a hardy plant that can grow outdoors in colder temperatures and even on mountainsides with almost no protection, thanks to the indica-influenced structure and the resulting durability. It also can do well without many nutrient feedings and as such, can be a good strain for those with a rookie, sparse, starter grow op and not much money to spend. However, like all of us, she still needs a little TLC from time to time, so don't expect her to give back if you don't spend a little energy making sure she's happy; keeping good ventilation in the grow room will strengthen that structure further and if you're growing outdoors, be sure to watch out for mold and pest problems. Within 11 weeks you should be able to harvest 600 to 700 grams of premium bud per square yard of grow space.

The smoke of The Bulldog Haze is a hard hitter, and one that tends towards indica effects as well as sativa. Both body and mind will feel weighty and relaxed, and this feeling is one that will last a good long while, so don't expect to be fully energized after a wake 'n bake. Certainly don't toke and then accidentally go to an energetic yoga class and then attempt to stay awake or keep up. It's happened to me before.

The Elephant Magic

With a name like this, how can you resist? Spain-based Dr. Canem and Company, breeders of Bull Terriers and the awesomely titled strain Cogollon Powell, have done it again with The Elephant Magic, a cross between Chocolate Thai and Original Haze from Sacred Seeds.

Parent plant Chocolate Thai is a famous strain from the 60s that began as a landrace plant in Southeast Asia, while Original Haze emerged a decade later as a mix of Mexican, Colombian, Thai and Indian plants. Their offspring enjoys a long flowering period of about 14 weeks, and is a more challenging strain than many intermediate growers are used to. Come harvest time, your plants won't be collapsing under the weight of their own buds, but once dried, you'll see why many experienced cultivators consider this plant to be well worth the effort.

The Elephant Magic's name hints at its psychoactive qualities, and the high retains the famous effects of Original Haze; uplifting, euphoric and quite psychedelic. The Haze influence bringing a spicy but sweet flavor to the mix, but you won't have much time to dwell on this, though, as the room starts dancing and wriggling around you and you have a hard time figuring out where your mouth actually is.

Dr. Canem and Company, Spain

Sativa-Dominant

Genetics: Original Haze x Chocolate Thai

Potency: THC 16%

facebook.com/drcanem

The Magician

De Sjamaan, based in Holland, has been in business since 1998 but has only recently begun producing lines of feminized and auto-flowering strains for a captive audience. This strain, excitingly named The Magician, promises to act as a living flashback to the first Skunk plants, which were more highly sativa-based and as such gave fantastic head highs. To achieve this, De Sjamaan have crossed Orange Skunk, which has the legendary Skunk #1 in its family, and Amsterdam coffeeshop favorite, White Widow.

A plant that is best grown indoors, The Magician manages to exhibit sativa traits without having too much stretch or growing too leggy. Plants will grow to around 5 feet without being too imposing, but show their sativa genes in the long buds that they produce. Later in the flowering stage these buds begin shimmering with crystals, bringing a welcome amount of "bling" to your grow room!

Be prepared for a bit of time travel when you spark up a stinky joint of The Magician; you'll be whisked back to the 70s when Skunk was Skunk and hair was long and greasy. The fruity smoke will lift you up and deposit you into a happy, hippy headspace that will make you feel that you were born thirty years too late and that your parents probably had it pretty good at your age. Why isn't NASA doing this kind of experimentation?

De Sjamaan, Holland

Sativa-Dominant

Genetics: Orange Skunk x White Widow

Potency: THC 19%

sjamaan.com

V2.0

You'd be forgiven for thinking that this Spanish seed company is the newest enterprise of Dr. Spock – and for all I know, it is. But even if the Vulkania office doesn't employ Bones and Captain Kirk, it's still impressive on many levels, as the Canary Islands-based company is consistently bringing out innovative new strains that combine popular varieties with new genetics. One of these is V2.0, a cross between New York City Diesel and an unknown strain that might just be from another galaxy. V2.0 is a fantastic sativa-dominant hybrid whose name still sounds distinctly Trekky to me. The plot thickens.

NYC Diesel is a U.S. strain that comprises a whole host of great genetics, from ChemDawg to Hawaiian and Afghani, and is a proven winner and a great choice for any breeding stock. By combining this with their own secret strain, Vulkania have created a 70/30 sativa-indica hybrid with all the vigor you'd expect from such a union and a strong sativa effect in the smoke. The NYC Diesel's relatively short stature keeps this strain from growing too tall, but it will need some tough love in the later stages of the vegetative phase if you don't want a 6-foot monster on your hands. It is much more suited to outdoor grows then indoor ones and will thank you for the extra space it can enjoy when planted out in the fresh air.

Vulkania Seeds, Spain

Sativa-Dominant

Genetics: NYC Diesel x Unknown Strain

Potency: THC 23%

vulkaniaseeds.com

If you're lucky enough to have a safe and secure grow space outside that's out of the view of police or prying potheads, you can plant V2.0 in April and be harvesting in September with a sizable yield. It's important to note that this strain needs a growth time of 3 weeks and a pre-flowering period of 14 days before it can be flipped into flower. By the end of the flowering stage your plants will start to look as if they're hatching little alien babies, as the buds express foxtailing traits, which is also known as crowning. This makes the nugs look like they've got lots of little feelers out probing for, well, whatever aliens probe for, but in fact this means that your crop is getting ready to be harvested. When the trichomes are fully loaded and starting to turn amber, around 65 days after flowering starts, it's time to beam them up, Scotty – or rather, chop them down, Buddy. Ahem.

It's hard to bring yourself to smoke up such cool-looking buds, but you'll soon get over that and indeed over everything, as V2.0 will take you flying high over all your previous reality and almost into the stratosphere. This one is a hard hitter, so it won't take long before you're totally spaced out, exploring the final frontier.

Violet Thai

The fantastic OtherSide Farms team are based in the U.S., and are on a mission to teach the world about medical marijuana. As well as grow classes and fantastic information, they dispense some wicked strains, including a few of their own creations like this Violet Thai. The genetics originally come from the beautiful island of Ko Chang in Thailand, which sits right on the border with Myanmar just off the west coast of the country. OtherSide Farms have stabilized this strain in order to bring it to their patients, as the THC content is one of the highest of any cannabis variety in the world, making it great medicine for those who need it.

With such genuine Thai genetics, this strain was always going to be one of those gorgeously tropical cannabis plants, and it doesn't disappoint on this front. Violet Thai grows as a very tall plant, with lots of those telltale sativa leaves: long and pointy with serrated edges. Despite being so obviously sativa in appearance, this plant only takes 11 weeks to be fully finished, unlike the 13 to 14 week flowering times of some other pure sativa strains. This makes it all the more unique and easy to grow. Although it can be grown indoors, its sheer size means that an outdoor grow will always be preferable. If growing indoors, be sure to keep good ventilation at all times, as this encourages stronger stem growth which will help later in the flowering stages. Even when growing outside, some LST can be helpful, otherwise by the time harvest rolls around you might find yourself unable to reach the top branches to check if the buds are done! The heat of its natural climate means that it has also grown very resistant to mold, which is great news for both indoor and outdoor growers.

OtherSide Farms, USA

Pure Sativa

Genetics: Pure Violet Thai

Potency: THC 22.3%

othersidefarms.com

Violet Thai has become well known and certainly well loved in its native area, especially among OtherSide Farms' loyal medicinal patients. The most loved thing about this strain is not its size or its yield, but its potency and its ability to treat pain, anxiety and lack of appetite. Boasting one of the highest THC contents in the world, this is a great medical strain and gives a very, very energetic effect that lasts seemingly forever. Though this might make you feel a little scattered if you overindulge, the right amount can get you dancing through the day like one of those irritating people who always says they're "high on life." I've been high on life, and it was alright, but I much prefer being high on weed. This can be a difficult strain to get hold of if you're not lucky enough to live in California, but never, ever miss the chance to try this strain if you can get it!

Virus

Spain's North of Seeds were one of the first medical marijuana seedbanks to open in their area of Spain, and since they did so, they have gained a reputation both locally and abroad for good quality and customer service. The team takes particular care to ensure that their seeds reach you in the best possible condition, keeping their seeds at exactly 6 degrees Celsius (42.8 degrees Fahrenheit) and dating each package so you can be sure of its freshness. This attention to detail has made these guys a hit with medical users, and with a strain as good as Virus, these guys are going to get even more popular! Virus is a fantastic cross between the company's Atomic +, an indica-dominant plant that looks and hits like a sativa, and a secret but potent sativa-dominant hybrid from the vaults of the breeders. This union has resulted in a beautiful-looking plant with deep green leaves and a high that hits like a freight train.

The good news for indoor growers is that this plant, unlike some sativa hybrids, can be tamed to grow in a greenhouse or an indoor grow room without too much effort. Though it will grow to be large, training and trimming can keep it at a manageable size. Another plus for both indoor and outdoor cultivators is its high resistance to mildew, a trait that it shares with its Atomic + parent. The upshot of this is that if you're growing in a similar climate to that of the south of Spain, or if you're cultivating many plants in a greenhouse, high humidity shouldn't cause you too many problems – although you should always aim for good air circulation within your grow area as this will strengthen your plants as well as make it difficult for mold and mildew to form. The Atomic + parent flowers in 55 days, and Virus blooms just a little later at 60 to 70 days. If growing outside, look to harvest on October 10th. With enough space and light, Virus plants can yield up to 600 grams of dried bud per square yard, and this figure rises to 700 grams per plant when grown outdoors: a huge yield in anyone's books!

North of Seeds, Spain

Sativa-Dominant

Genetics: Atomic + x

Unknown Sativa

Potency: THC 15-18%

northofseeds.com

You might be somewhat confused when you smoke your first bowl of Virus, because although it doesn't look or taste like magic mushrooms, it sure as hell feels like it. The intense fruity smell will leave you nice and refreshed for the debilitating, highly psychoactive high that's about to smack you right in the brain. This is, however, a very welcome experience, and you won't be left with that part-grin, part-grimace you get after six hours of a mushroom trip, as this will slide nicely into a relaxing stone so you can recover with a stack of cookies.

Vortex

Team Green Avengers and their main breeder, Subcool, are known in the cannabis seed community as good guys: honest about their strains and quick to give customer support when it's needed. They're also known for their interesting strains, and Vortex is no different in that regard. As a mix of Apollo 13 and Space Queen via Querkle, this is one of those plants that manages both quality and quantity at the same time.

Like most of us, Vortex is happiest in a warmer climate and doesn't mind whether it's indoors or outdoors. With just a little convincing, it can be grown well in ScrOG set ups, and takes well to both hydro and soil grows, though you should be careful of mold developing in their hotter environment. This is a very stable hybrid, and gives great-looking plants that should be forced to flower after 60 days and harvested 60 days after that.

Subcool says that the aroma is one of rotten fruit and baby poo, which doesn't exactly sound appealing, but it seems as if Vortex is the durian of the weed world: disgusting to smell but delicious to taste. It also has the added bonus of getting you totally baked off your face; no matter how illegal durian is in public places, I don't imagine that eating too much would leave you tripping balls and smiling like a demon.

Subcool and Team
Green Avengers, USA
Sativa-Dominant
Genetics: Apollo 13 x
Querkle
Potency: THC 18.08%
tgagenetics.com

Waipi'o Hapa

Even though Hawaii is the 4th smallest state in the U.S., it still houses a hell of a lot of good cannabis genetics. There are several of these landrace sativa strains featured in this very book, and Waipi'o Hapa is one of the rarer types. America's Centennial Seeds due to popular demand, are offering the seeds once more.

Originally from the Waipi'o Valley on the North Shore of the Big Island, this strain was stabilized by Centennial Seeds and the F2 females averaged a height of around 5.5 feet. The flowering time, too, is on the short side for a pure strain, sitting at around the 8- or 9-week mark. These plants are strong in both structure and temperament, and have both sturdy growth patterns and minimal sensitivity to nutrient and pH drift. They also have a wide canopy all the way down their stalks, with many bud sites.

These plants are pretty heavy duty, and give heavy yields of buds that smell like the Singapore Botanical Gardens: full of lime, hibiscus and fresh waterfalls. A pure sativa all the way, the smoke will leave you hugely stimulated and unable to stay in one place, so pack a bowl of Waipi'o Hapa when you wake up and everyone will think you've turned over an impressively productive new leaf. Little will they know that you're actually high as a North Shore wave during the Eddie.

Centennial Seeds, USA

Pure Sativa

Genetics: Landrace Hawaiian

Potency: THC 12%

centennialseeds.com

Western Winds

Holland's Sagarmatha Seeds (which is so-called after the Nepalese name for Mount Everest, in case you didn't know) have been in the game for long enough to make them one of Amsterdam's big players. Their strains always turn heads, and Western Winds was no exception when it was first announced to the world. A sativa-heavy hybrid, it's been kept as Sagarmatha's breeding stock for a while now and is fully stabilized and easy to grow outdoors. The breeders consider it to be one of their best ever sativa projects, and it's similar to Kali Mist and certain types of Haze in that it grows like a college basketball player but smokes like a high school dropout.

I've heard it said that Western Winds does well under a 12/12 lighting regime right from the start, but as I've never tried this, I can't recommend it myself. It does do well, however, in organic soil grows with additional worm castings, and exhibits perfectly fine without any expensive nutrients or labor-intensive training. However, this is one that's suited more to an outdoor garden, so growing inside isn't impossible but will take a little more work on the part of the grower. Pruning the top a couple of times will stop it growing out of the top of your house, and it might need additional support from stakes near harvest due to the weight of the buds. Then again, the plant's doing all the hard work, so you can't really complain, can you?

Sagarmatha Seeds, Holland

Sativa-Dominant

Genetics: Unknown Sativa

Potency: THC 18%

sagarmatha.nl

The vegetative period of this plant isn't set in stone, but instead is finished when the plants have between 4 and 7 internodes ready to sprout. Its average height will be around 5 feet or a little higher and the finished buds will be long and very resinous: a beautiful payoff if you've been struggling to keep the plant tamed. After the flowering time of 75 days, which is definitely longer than some sativas, but is well worth the wait, you should be able to bring in a harvest of up to 350 grams per square yard of grow room. That's a great harvest in anyone's book, and thankfully it's not a case of quantity over quality either, as these are some seriously dank nugs.

Though this strain is called Western Winds, the finished buds have an Oriental flavor that's definitely set in the East. The high has been described both as spiritual and as a party high, so I guess you get whatever you want, but either way it's a crazy stone that's very invigorating and great for keeping you up all night. Even the staff at Sagarmatha say that Western Winds is their favorite weed, so put that in your pipe and smoke it. No, really, do!

White Haze

Based in Amsterdam, White Label Seeds are a well-respected seed company who've improved on many classic strains through their fantastic breeding programs. One of these improved strains is White Haze, which is a variation of one of the most popular sativas, Haze. Though they're keeping the genetic formation of this strain under their hat (and understandably so), we know that the original Haze was a pure sativa blend of Colombian, Mexican, Thai and Indian genetics with massive growth and huge sparkling colas. As a member of the Haze family, White Haze has kept the crystalline buds and the vigor, but with some indica influence the nugs have filled out on the inside and now give a balanced head and body high that some say is even better than a Haze high.

Two of the main problems with growing pure sativas like Haze are the size of the plants and the flowering times. Sativas, especially landrace sativas, can grow extremely large, making them both unsuitable for indoor growing and a nightmare to look after even outdoors. By bringing an indica influence to the sativa genetics, White Label have tamed the growth of Haze without compromising on the yield. The maximum height of White Haze sits around the 6-foot mark, so although the plants aren't exactly at the Danny DeVito stature, they're capable of being grown indoors or in a greenhouse and can be kept even smaller with training and topping. The presence of indica genetics also brings the flowering time to a more acceptable level, and keeps the vegetative stage shorter than normal with a Haze. Careful growers can keep the height at a Tom Cruise level, or, if they're lucky, a Michael J. Fox.

White Label Seeds, Holland

Sativa-Dominant

Genetics: Unknown Haze hybrid

Potency: THC 18%

whitelabelseeds.com

50 to 70 days after you force those bad boys into flowering, you should be able to swipe a harvest of around 125 grams per plant, depending on how high your plants stand. When growing, you should decide what your priority is; if it is yield, let them grow bigger, but if it is ease and space, keep them small. Either way, you'll get a solid stash that's covered in resin glands and shines like a movie star's teeth.

There's a reason that people go through the rigmarole of growing the tallest, most space-hogging sativa strains, and that's because the high is absolutely phenomenal. White Label knows this, and they've managed to maintain this trait even when introducing indica genetics. The soaring, brainy high is pure sativa, and the taste will leave you in no doubt that this is a Haze. Yet the weight in your eyelids is a little prod from the indica that says it's still there – and that's what makes White Haze a definite winner.

Wisconsin Flame

This 60/40 sativa-indica hybrid, produced by an unknown but very talented grower/breeder in Wisconsin, was created back in the heady days of 2006 and combines genetics from a landrace sativa, native to Wisconsin, and the indica-dominant Amsterdam Flame from Holland's Paradise Seeds.

A plant for more experienced growers rather novice cultivators, Wisconsin Flame grows best indoors in soil or hydro setups, particularly deep water culture grow ops, in which it enjoys a longer vegetative period and gives absolutely huge plants. Reaching a height of 5 to 6 feet, it is not suitable for ScrOG growing but will flourish well if cuttings are vegetated for 2 to 3 weeks then flowered into full-size plants. Humidity in the dark period should be lower than 50% to help prevent rot, and as it takes longer to ripen than many strains, microdeficiencies can be common. To combat this, provide a well-balanced mix of absorbable nutrients, then flush during the last 10 days of flowering with ½ teaspoon of molasses per gallon of water. The resulting yield will be heavy and clean.

Unidentified Wisconsin Grower, USA
Sativa-Dominant
Genetics: Wisconsin Native Landrace Sativa (Kenosha) x Amsterdam Flame
Potency: THC 22%

Due to the fairly balanced nature of this plant's genetics, the smoke gives a high that affects both the head and the body, and relaxes both. The smoke is deliciously mango-like and fresh; this is one to sit down with and enjoy properly!

Yummy

Since their beginnings in a grow shop in Barcelona ten years ago, the breeders at Resin Seeds have been immersed in cannabis cultivation for quite some time. In the last few years they've taken their wealth of experience and information, and put these to work breeding original strains like Yummy. This variety was created by introducing a Yumbolt female, from Sagarmatha, to Soma's G-13 Haze stud, and these two plants fell in love faster than Shakespeare's star-crossed lovers but with a lot less family drama. The Yumbolt plant came from a clone of a fantastic mother plant kept since the 90s, and was pollinated with the G-13 Haze male in order to produce some regular seeds of beautiful offspring. The result of their union was then narrowed down to a couple from hundreds of F1s to produce the feminized Yummy seeds now available.

Nothing ever works out perfectly in any love story, and the first flush of Yumbolt and G-13 Haze's first kids expressed two main different phenotypes; one more indica-leaning, with a taste of strawberries and sugar and a high yield, and one more sativa-dominant with a Hazey smoke. The breeders picked a phenotype that was somewhere in between these two, which grew like an indica but still had that special Haze hint. The plant we get these days still expresses these traits, and grows with one main cola and few side branches.

Resin Seeds, Spain

Sativa-Dominant

Genetics: Yumbolt x G-13 Haze

Potency: THC 19-23%

resinseeds.net

Yummy is an easy strain to grow, and when grown indoors is ready in just under 10 weeks. When grown outdoors in the Northern Hemisphere, she's usually ready for harvest at the start of October. Be careful towards the later stages of flowering, as she can tend to stretch if the lights are kept too close to her, causing stress, and this will upset the look of your crop and make it less stable. When she's almost fully mature the buds will have orange, yellow and pale green colorings and along with the deep green leaves, they certainly will look Yummy. Don't get carried away though; they're to smoke, not eat!

The sweet pine taste of this strain comes through once your buds have cured and you've packed a nice fat bowl, but you'll also get that hint of spicy Haze taste that always lingers on the palette. The smoke is thick and the high is so cerebral you feel your brain trying to pop right out the top of your skull. Given the name, this might be a good strain to cook up into some brownies and get super baked, but I've never been able to keep my hands off the stash long enough to make the butter. If you can resist the Yummy smoke, let me know how the brownies go!

Zoid Fuel

The Wizards of Oz are a new collective of Australian breeders including Wally Duck and the underground breeding star Moonunit. As if sharing a name with Frank Zappa's kid isn't cool enough, in his brilliantly-named Zoid Fuel, Moonunit has created a heavy sativa hybrid which is interesting for its lack of any North American or European lineage. With Asian influence on the pure Australian genetics of Moonunit's Fuel line, Zoid Fuel definitely stands out from the crowd, and is a testament to Moonunit's tireless efforts to bring high-quality and very exciting Australian strains to the wider community. I salute you for your efforts!

A "bush plant" bred and homogenized to be grown indoors, Zoid Fuel takes very well to amended soil. The breeders have worked hard to reduce the flowering time of this line and as such, this plant should be fully finished in about 9 to 12 weeks. As a bush plant, this strain, like most Australians I've met, much prefers being outdoors and will be energized and revitalized by the natural light until its almost glowing with life. It might even get a tan if you're lucky. The plants are very responsive to light, so if you're growing indoors you should keep an sharp eye on how close they are growing to the bulbs, and move the light source accordingly – movable lights are a great investment before starting to grow this strain. Midway through the vegetative stage is the best time to push the growth with a healthy dose of nutrients, though this should be slowed down once flowering starts. The myriad tastes of this strain are one

The Wizards of Oz, Australia

Sativa-Dominant

Genetics: Papua New Guinea Gold x Australian Bush Sativa x Chinese Indica

of its greatest traits, so be sure not to use any synthetic nutrients towards the end of flowering and do a good flush with blackstrap molasses for 2 weeks before the cut. It would be a travesty to lose that taste to a chemically flavor.

A pleasant plethora of tastes including the mad mix of fuel, mint and incense, Zoid Fuel is much tastier than it sounds. Even if you've been smoking other strains all night long, once you light up a blunt of this, it will cut straight through the haze of other smoke and hit you right between the eyes. The smoke of this bud gives a typical sativa high that comes through in waves, getting more intense with every break, just like a Gold Coast surf trip. Starting in your head, it will move through your body and give you energy and enough gab to keep on talking all night long – and when you're done you can soak up the Aussie vibes by watching *Riding Giants* or even *Point Break,* if you're high enough to put up with Keanu Reeves' acting.

PHOTOS BY WIZARDS OF OZ

Index

Index

Index

Index